ARISE

&

SHINE

ARISE
&
SHINE

Becoming God's Shining Star When the People
Need Light the Most

"Arise and shine, for thy light is come and the glory
of the Lord is raised upon thee"

{Isaiah 61:1-2}

REV. ALFRED JOHNSON MENSAH

authorHOUSE®

AuthorHouse™ LLC
1663 Liberty Drive
Bloomington, IN 47403
www.authorhouse.com
Phone: 1-800-839-8640

Published by AuthorHouse 04/04/2014

ISBN: 978-1-4969-0100-2 (sc)
ISBN: 978-1-4969-0099-9 (e)

Library of Congress Control Number: 2014906043

CONTENTS

DEDICATION

This book is affectionately dedicated to God Almighty who snatched me from the flaming fire of Satan and has brought me from a place of disgrace to a perpetual place of grace through the light of our Lord Jesus Christ which raised upon me from the cross of Calvary over 2000 years ago.

ACKNOWLEDGEMENT

It is from the very core of my heart that I wish to render my gratitude sincerely to the following dignitaries whose foresight, vision, love, encouragement and ocean of inspiration master minded that arrived of this maiden book.

First and foremost, I give all to the Most High God and His Son Jesus Christ, the Savior and the Precious Holy Spirit whose guardianship resulted to the accomplishment of this goal. Having said that, I wish to acknowledge Apostle Alfred Adams of Church of Reconciliation for his persistent prayer, inspiration and love. Furthermore, I appreciate Prophet Kofi Owusu, Owner of Holy Fire Dynamic for his fervent prayers. I personally salute Rev. Tony Sarkodie of Elshaddai Assemblies of God Ministry for his words of encouragement and love. Similarly, I sincerely thank these men of God namely Elder Derick Mensah, Elder William Aduamoah for their prayers and other support services.

Finally, I graciously thank my parents namely Mr. and Mrs. Owusu, as well as the rest of my entire family for their prayers.

May Jehovah Elohini, bless you all in the mighty name of Jesus. Amen.

Pastor Alfred

INTRODUCTION

This has been a mission accomplished for me because the Lord Jesus has tremendously endowed me with great insight to hardship His holy people {Israel} went through in the hands of their enemies and the restoration of His holy city Jerusalem to send a message through this book to the people of this generation of darkness who really need the light of our Lord Jesus Christ. The devil has brought a very thick darkness upon the earth but the good news is that our Lord Jesus Christ has come with a great light to destroy the works of the devil

In Isaiah chapters 60-62, the picture depicts again s Isaiah describes the future glory of Jerusalem in the millennial kingdom, Zion, another for the holy city of Jerusalem and the chosen people of God, the Jews, is told to wake up. She is urged to look and see the glory of her future fulfilled blessings during the millennium, after Christ returns and sets his kingdom on earth with its capitol in Jerusalem. He continued to declare that nations that persecuted Israel will in that day honor and serve her{ the new Jerusalem}, and Jesus presence will transform not only the city but also her people. And this is what the Lord has promised to do on you if only you will pay heed to this divine call.

God repeats His promise to avenge and comfort His people in chapter 61, verses 1-3
The land of Israel and its people will be restored {61:4-9} as God clothes Zion in "garment of salvation" {61:10}. In Isaiah 62:1, God once again announces that He will continue to work on Jerusalem's behalf until her righteousness, salvation, and glory are recognized by

the rest of the world. Her restoration has been guaranteed {62:2-7} by the promise and the power of God. And the good part of it was that Isaiah foresees a great crowd awaiting the approach of Jesus Christ to the Holy City of Jerusalem {62:10-11}. And the greatest wonder of all is that these people, the inhabitants of the Zion in this time, will be called "the Holy People" for all will be redeemed by our Lord Jesus Christ{62:12}.

One of the most persistent themes of Old Testament prophecies teaches that at history's end or before the end of this world, God will set up on earth and the messiah will rule over all the nations of the world. In the Old Testament bright vision of the future, the kingdoms comes following God's crushing defeat of all evil and the great spiritual conversion of the Jews which then leads to the conversion of a great number of gentiles, as well. There are a great number of passages expressing the Old Testament prophet's vision of this coming glorious kingdom. The picture created in Isaiah 60:19,20 is similar to the one we see in Revelation 21-22. Isaiah 60 describes the dawning of a new day. Isaiah made certain things clear and let's have a look at them.

"ARISE AND SHINE" is God's wake up call to Jerusalem in verse 1 because a new day is dawning for Israel. This light is not from the sun but from the glory of God shining on the city. God's glory had once dwelt in the tabernacle according to Exodus 40-34-38, only to depart because of Israel's sin {1Samuel 4:21}. God's glory then came into the temple, according to 1 Kings 8:11, but it departed when the nation turned to worshipping idols. The glory then came to Israel in the person of Jesus Christ {John 1:14}, but the nation nailed it to the cross.

For it says "YOUR LIGHT HAS COME"—Jesus Christ, our light, has come. He came, He died, He rose again. He has already won the victory on the cross and all sin has been paid for. We are on the winning side! This is more than enough reason to live for Him and shine. The light of Christ shines upon to make you a special person or agent of God on earth.

"THE GLORY OF THE LORD HAS RISEN ON YOU" Jesus has given his own life to you. His presence is with and in the believer. This makes all the difference. There is no way we can shine without him. But we have no longer have to be trapped in the frustration of living with only our own resources. Naturally, we all failed as a result of the sins committed by Adam and Eve. But we can shine through His life in us. We all have fears but are we meant to just throw in the towel and live in the fear or are there now the hope and opportunity to arise and shine because of the Lord's presence in our life? Of course there is! We have every reason to shine because of the glory of God which has risen upon us and we are now fearful to the devil and not the other way round so begin to get up as a shining star.

"PEOPLE ARE IN DARKNESS" we are also urged to arise and shine because people in this dispensation are living in total darkness. As a matter of fact, this is deep or gross darkness to be precise. Remember this passage is prophetic of the end of the age. Darkness will cover the entire earth. There is a lot of darkness hovering on the horizon. The generation is loosing its values morally, spiritually, financially, emotionally and so on in a very faster pace. In so many areas there is the darkness of despair hovering over this world. The one good thing is that the darker it becomes, the easier it is to see the light. And Isaiah said in the previous chapter, he noted that; "when the enemy comes in like a flood, the Spirit of the Lord will raise up a standard against him"

"NATIONS WILL COME TO YOUR LIGHT" the final reason to arise and shine is the result: This is scientifically true. Light attracts even animals and this is what Isaiah was referring to. He said; "Gentiles shall come to your light". The light attracts—and not just moths. People want to see something that is real. Although as someone said—"some people change their ways when the see the light, others only when they feel the heat" let the light of Christ in you draw men to His glory by leading an exemplary life of Christ on earth.

CHAPTER 1
THE NEW DAWN HAS COME

INTRODUCTION

As explain in the introductory part of the book, the Jerusalem's captivity had been Israel's darkest moment in their history, but in a plain language that is not the darkness Isaiah was referring to. He was rather describing the awful darkness that will cover the earth during the day of the Lord as stated in {Amos 5:18} when God punishes the nations of the earth for their sins {Isaiah 2:12; 13:6}. But the prophet is also describing the glorious light that will come to Israel when her Messiah returns to reign in Jerusalem. When he said, "the earth shall be filled the knowledge of the glory of the Lord, as the waters covers the seas" According to Habakkuk 2:14}, Israel sons and daughters who have accepted Christ as their personal Lord and Savior will come home again {Isaiah 60:4. 8-9} and all of them will know the Lord

It will be dawning of a new day for the nations of the world as well as Israel, The Gentiles will come to Jerusalem to worship the Lord and to share the wealth. Isaiah sees ships and caravans bringing people and wealth to Jerusalem from all over the world {60:5-7}; and the nations that refuse to honor and obey the Lord and His city will be judged by Him {60:12}. Even Israel old enemies will see the light and help to serve the Lord {60: 10, 14}. Thank God for his Son Christ Jesus through whom you and I are called to be part of this, glorious, and joyous moment which is coming soon. For the purpose of this chapter, let us remind ourselves once again on how Isaiah itemized his prophecy as discussed in the introduction for better understanding.

ARISE, SHINE: The subject of the address does not distinctly appear until Isaiah 60:14, where it is found to be "the city of the Lord, the Zion of the Holy one of Israel" Zion has long been prostrate in the dust from the prophet's standpoint, and cover with thick darkness. Now she is bidden to "arise and shine like a day". You have slept for too long in your sins and you turned a deaf ear to the word of God for far too long. For how long do you want to remain in your failure? Get up and gather momentum and begin shine within the radiance of God's greatest light in the person of Christ Jesus.

FOR THE LIGHT IS COME: Zion could not shine with her own light, for she has no light of her own, having preferred to "walk in darkness" {Isaiah 59:9} but she may reflect the radiance which streams from the person of Jesus Christ, whose glory is risen upon her, "In thy light shall we see light" {Psalm 36:9}. After failing miserably in life trying to do it on your own, why don't you give it all up unto Him? The truth of the matter is that you cannot do it on your own without this great light. You need Jesus to show you the way because he is the light of the world, {John 1:4}

"FOR BEHOLD, THE DARKNESS SHALL COVER THE EARTH": As in Egypt, a "thick darkness" covered the whole land at word of Moses {Exodus 10:22}, while still "the children of Israel had light in their dwellings" so now the world and "the nations of the world lay a deep obscurity, into which scarcely a ray of light penetrated, while on Israel, there dawned a glory which streamed from the throne of God, and at once transfigured her, and gave her the appearance of an angel of the Most High. In the radiance of this light she was to stand up and show herself, and then great results would follow.

Chapter 60-62 are the heart of the third section of Isaiah {56-66}. The community of returned exiles struggled to believe that God was still working in their midst. They began to wander where is God? Isaiah{59:1-21}. The promises recorded in the second section of Isaiah during the exile {40:55} pointed to a great future for God's people. They had gained the possession of the land as promised. But the reality is that they were barely existing. The community of God's people was in no condition to be a light to the nations {42: 5-7}

Throughout of these chapters, prophetic interpretations of actual historical events are interwoven with visionary descriptions of the working out of God's purpose in history. The language in this chapter is highly poetic, painting a glorious word picture of the restoration of Jerusalem {check Micah 4, Ezekiel 40}.

Not a single promise of God upon your life will fail to manifest upon your life because He sent His only begotten Son to come and die in order to get you out of slavery market of sin. All He requires of you is to pay attention to His voice and come to His everlasting light and glory.

HISTORICAL CONTEXT OF THE FALLEN JERUSALEM

The story of Israel's captivity to the land of Babylon is one of the heart breaking and traumatic stories of all time. A great number of men, women and even infants of Israel were killed in the process. The walls of the great city were destroyed and twelve gates were not spared. The entire nation became desolated, all these as a result of the sins of the people. After a long struggle and severe opposition from surrounding peoples, the returned exiles finally won support from the Persian king Artaxerxes.

When the time came for God's redemption to be shown to His people, the king commissioned Ezra the scribe to return to Jerusalem to secure the welfare of the city. Artaxerxes funded Ezra's mission and ordered the provincial treasures to provide Ezra whatever he needed. {You can check that from Ezra 7; Isaiah 60:5-7}. Specifically, mention is the intention to "beautify the house of the Lord in Jerusalem"{Ezra 7:27; note Isaiah

60:13}. The Lord Himself had finished dealing with His people and it was within his time frame to restore them back to a more befitting place than the former.

The fact is that the returned exiles faced severe problems. Part of the reason was that the people had allowed sin to pervert their mission as God's people {Isaiah 59}. In chapter 60, the prophet renewed the promises of a new day for the community of faith. He assures the people that God has not forgotten them and their mission as a light to the world has not changed. The new events transpiring mark the beginning of God's new day for his people. This is exactly the plan of God upon your life. He knows your sins and understands your weakness. Nothing is too late to repair; all that He needs from you is your receptive heart and a new mindset towards His glorious light is risen upon you. And trust me; your life will not remain the same if you pay heed to His voice. And if you do this, this is going to be the divine promise of God upon your life.

15 "Although you have been forsaken and hated, with no one traveling through, I will make you the everlasting pride and joy of all generations. 16, you will drink the milk of nations and be nursed at royal breasts. Then you will know that I, the LORD, am your savior and redeemer, the Mighty one of Jacob. 17, instead of bronze, I will bring you gold, and silver in place of iron, instead of wood I will bring you bronze, and iron in place of stones. I will make peace your governor and righteousness your ruler. 18, no longer will violence be heard in your hand, nor ruin or destruction within your borders, but you will call your walls Salvation and your gates Praise, "Isaiah 60: 15-18}.

THE GOSPEL DEPICTS A SPECIAL REVELATION OF GOD'S GLORY

The prophet made us to understand that the light that has come to the world is the glory of God. And if that is the case, what then is "the glory of God"? We take the which the Eternal Father gave to the request of

Moses which the bible says; "I beseech Thee, show me Thy Glory," the reply He gave was not, I will show the infinitude of My possessions, the boundless of My dominions, the almightiness of My power, the immeasurable depths of My wisdom, but it was rather; "I will cause My goodness to pass before thee," What a wonderful God we serve! And the gospel indeed is a wonderful revelation of God's goodness, in the form of amazing mercy towards a guilty world. God is God of second chance and He wants you to renew your mind towards Him so that He will have the access in your life to show you his everlasting goodness and mercies. Let us look at how the glory of His goodness, work on our salvation

The glory of His goodness is seen in the gift of His Son. The bible makes it a sparkling clear that, "He spared not His own Son". The greatest mystery behind the whole thing is that if God did not withhold His only Son against our salvation, what else will be so difficult for Him to do for you? The glory of His goodness is seen in the entire history of His Son. All the compassion, the tender love and mercy, which Christ displayed when on earth, were the reflected rays of infinite goodness of His Father.

THE GOSPEL IMPOSES A SPECIAL OBLIGATION UPON US

Let us consider the two primary words in the prophecy; "Arise, Shine."

a. ARISE:—It is a special command from God which simply means do not sleep while the rays of divine goodness are streaming on you. God is not encouraging you to get up from your slumber and make your hay while the sun shines. In order words, it means arise to thought, to penitence, to gratitude, to worship. Arise, discharge the duties and enjoy the advantages of a day flooded with the sun of mercy

b. SHINE:—Reflect the rays of this goodness. Let this love of God be so "shed abroad in thy heart," that it streams forth its radiance in thy every action, and bless the circle in which thou lives. Do not be as opaque body, obstructing the rays and throwing a shadow over thy sphere; but be a mirror, to reflect every falling beam. This is your time to shine because God Himself says so. He has given you the privilege to arise and shine in this dark world. Shine with the gospel of Christ. Shine with testimony of your salvation. And shine with the beauty of Christ.

CHRIST JESUS IS THE LIGHT OF THE WORLDS

The words of the text comprise an exhortation to "arise" and "shine"; and a reason to enforce it,—"thy light is come, the glory of the Lord is risen upon thee".

1. THE REASON, there is such a connection between ignorance and darkness, that the one is constantly put for the other in scripture. If ignorance is termed darkness, so knowledge is properly compared to light. At the dawn of day, the traveler takes fresh courage; he perceives the path in which he should go, and proceeds on it rejoicing. In the same manner, religious knowledge enlightens a man as to his true business in his life, and sets him to work out his salvation. And Christ is Sun which sends forth this religious knowledge. Let us look at two things the sun does in our lives.

1. THE SUN:—The sun when it rises in the morning, dispels all clouds and mists and dews, and shows every object in its true colors. So, without that light which Christ has furnished by His gospel, we cannot perceive those truths it is most needful we should perceive.

2. THE SUN:—when shines above us, does more than enlighten every object. It nourishes, it invigorates. Without it, the sickly plants drop and decay, and bring no fruit to perfection. And the effect of the sun upon outward nature is a striking emblem of the influence of Christ upon the heart. In Him is life, vigorous, spiritual life; and the life is the life of men. Having had Jesus as your sun for energy,

what are you waiting for? Just make a step and he will bring it to perfection.

THE EXHORTATION, "ARISE AND SHINE"

1. When the sun rises, and scatters the mists of night, he gives a summons to mankind to rise also, and set themselves to the discharge of their various duties. In the same manner, the appearance of Christ in the world is a summons to all who hear of His revelation, to, "arise". To awake out of the sleep of ignorance, the sleep of thoughtlessness, the sleep of sin, which are, in truth, the sleep of death; and to apply themselves, before "the night cometh in which no man can work," to the business which God has appointed them to perform both for themselves and for Him. You have slept for too long, get up and work for Christ.

2. The text requires that you not only "arise," but you "shine." That Christ has risen in the world is nothing, unless He illuminates your hearts also. When the sun is up, and shines brightly upon any object, that which before was dark shines too; receives brilliancy not its own, not natural to it. So is it likewise, when Christ illuminates the heart, it takes a new coloring, a light which by nature it had not. Enlightened by the gospel, the simple becomes wise, and acquires the knowledge which is most truly valuable—the knowledge of duty towards God and man. Enlightened by the gospel, he who was selfish and covetous is made liberal, and abounds in the feelings of brotherly kindness, and in the works of charity.

Enlightened by the gospel, he who was sensual becomes temperate and pure, and "let's his moderation be known by all men". The "lover of this world" becomes the "lover of God" and "sets his affections on things above". In this way the light which has shone above them is reflected in their conduct, and it is visible in their whole character. The sun shines; but some objects still continue to be dark and gloomy. Between them and the sun light, other objects interpose, and prevent his beams from shinning upon them. And so it is in the world of grace. The gospel of Christ has enlightened us, therefore He wants you and I to do the same to the world and bring them to the full knowledge of his divine light which is salvation through the gospel of Christ.

THE DAWNING OF GOD'S LIGHT IS A WAKE UP CALL

1. THE DAWNING OF THE LIGHT;—"thy light is come" If the light is always near, but the darkness is in man's heart and the blindness in his soul, we have to ask how the darkness passes away, and to point out the manner in which the glory of God dawns upon it, in order that we may see why it's dawning is a summons to arise and shine. There are three requisites for it's dawning-three stages in the history of the soul's enlightenment.

    a. Spiritual penitence
    b. Spiritual penitence must pass into spiritual love
    c. Spiritual love necessitates spiritual prayer

THE AWAKENING CALL "Arise and shine," that summons is the inevitable result of the dawning of the light. When God is felt to be near a man thus-in penitence, love, and prayer, the man is imperatively bound to reflect the glory which has risen in his heart; to bear witness of the light which has pierced and transformed his soul. Let us again observe that this is also is base on a great principle, thus the deepest emotion in a man's nature must reveal itself in his life. I proceed to show the way in which the glory of the Lord thus manifests itself in life.

    a. In the majesty of holiness
    b. In the beauty of unselfishness
    c. In the earnestness of your efforts for men

1. The voice speaks to individual. It is important for us to identify the voice of God when He speaks. How few even realize their possibilities. We have had religious training, we have been taught to consider all questions as they appear in relation to God, we have grown up in a religious atmosphere, and yet the consciousness that no man is a true man until he reflects Jesus Christ in words,

11. The voice of God comes to the church. The voice comes to both local and universal churches. The church realizes its true mission only as it reflects to the Divine light, which means, simply, realizes the life which was in Jesus Christ.

    a. The church should reflect Jesus in its worship. With Him worship was something essential, and vital. Before every great act of His career, He went apart from men to pray. The sources of His life were in God. Worship and prayer are the conduits along which flow streams of spiritual vitality. Is the church a praying Church? Then it is continuing the works of Christ.

    b. The church lives to repeat the teachings of Jesus Christ. Every word from the pulpit should be in line with the sound doctrine of Jesus Christ. Any other is classified as the doctrine of the devil thwart the foundation established by the Apostles, Jesus being the corner stone.

c. In like manner, the church should reflect Jesus in the service of humanity. It lives to continue His ministry. The most hospitable place in every community ought to be the Church of Jesus Christ. Has anyone a grief? Let him go to the Church. Are any lonely? Let them go to the Church. Has any disgraced themselves and their friends? Let them seek the Church and its help. But all these various classes find there a welcome? Not only within its walls, but outside also the Church should serve humanity in the spirit of Christ.

111. This cry of the Prophet comes to nations. This was for the nations, as well as individuals and Churches, exist to continue the incarnation. That nation has not begun to realize its possibilities which have not learnt that its superlative privilege is the manifestation of Jesus Christ. The function of government is not only the protection of the people, but also the service of the humanity. In the vision of the Prophet when the light broke upon the sides of Mount Zion the nations saw the glory and were attracted by it{verses 3, 14}.

ARISE, SHINE

1. To whom the charge is addressed:—To the Church of Christ. This is evident from the context. Further, it appears from the nature of the charge that it can apply only to the Church. There is none else on earth capable of at once fulfilling the charge. The world cannot, for it is essentially dark-"darkness covers the earth." The Church is compared to be reflected and acted as artificial lights. Christ enlightens the world through His Church.

11. The charge itself:—This a two-fold charge implying two distinct acts.

a. "Arise." This implies that the Church is in the meantime in a prostate conditions; her place is in the dust. This may be partly in penitence. It may indicate a state of affliction and mourning; the Church may be sitting in sackcloth. But chiefly, it implies a state of sloth, worldliness, and carnality. Whatever be the cause of this prostration the Church is directed to rise from the dust now.

b. "Shine." "Christ shall give thee the light," for this very purpose not merely to enlighten yourself, impart life and joy to you, but that you may "shine," and give light to world. And this applies both to the Church as whole and to the members of the Church individually. There are two ways in which those who have been enlightened by Christ may give light. On the one hand, by simply shining, each one in his sphere, as a separate light, perhaps in the midst of darkness. On the other hand, by kindling other lights.

111. The argument by which it is enforced:—"Thy light is come" the Church has no independent light of her own, and cannot shine of herself; and so, such an encouragement as this is needed. "Thy light"—this must mean Christ Himself, for He is the light of the Church. "Is come"—Christ did not come till seven or eight hundred years after this prophecy was delivered. But the prophecy refers to gospel times. Accordingly, the Church did arise and shine at that time more brightly and auspiciously than she had ever done before. We are really in the dark-age and this is the time the world needs the Church to shine and show its brightness of peace and hope to all men here on earth.

THE PROPHECY IS AN AROUSING CALL

There are some Christians who have wasted a large part of their lives for want of somebody or something to wake them up. There is more evil wrought in the world by want of thought than by downright malice, and there is more good left undone through want of thought than through any aversion to the doing of good. Some Christians, appear to have been born in the land of slumber, and they continue live in their native country of dreams. It does not matter where you come from and where you were born, you can arise and shine for God's glory if only you believe.

SHINING CHRISTIANS

1. God's own people, this is my message, remember your privilege. Your light has come. Therefore use it appropriately to glory the Lord.

   a. Recollect out of what darkness that light has delivered you.

   b. Remember this light which God has given you, in his own glory. God's face is mirrored in the sea; but there is not space enough for the face of Deity to be fully reflected in the broad Atlantic, or in all the oceans put together. The image of God is to be fully seen in Jesus Christ, and nowhere else; for there you behold attributes which creation cannot display.

   c. There is also this blessed thing to be said about the light; you will never lose it {Isaiah 60:20}

11. I want to rouse you to service. "Arise, Shine." Since your light has come, shine by

   a. By holy cheerfulness
   b. By a gracious godliness
   c. By zealous earnestness
   d. By a secret bravery

What else can we say apart from obeying God's voice to do His will? He has given us a second chance to prove ourselves worthy of His service. We should therefore guard this divine privilege jealously and do His will. Arise and Shine for this is your time to do exploit in Christ Jesus.

The Lord who brought the good people of Israel from their hopelessness to a perpetual place is ever ready to give you a helping hand to snatch you from the slavery market of sin and change your story from bitter to better.

CHAPTER 2

SHINING OVER YOUR FAILURES

This is one of the English words that almost everyone on earth hates to hear. No one will like to hear it around him or her in connection with anything he or she does. And if this word is that popular, then the question we should be asking ourselves is, what is failure? For the purpose of this discussion, let me help you with some few definitions at this point to see if it will help us to understand the concept better.

FAILURE IS;

1. An act of failing or proving unsuccessful; lack of success
2. Nonperformance of something due, required, or expected: a failure to success.
3. A subnormal quantity or quality; an insufficiency; the failures of crops.
4. Deterioration or decay, esp. of vigor or strength.
5. A condition of being bankrupt by reason of insolvency.
6. A becoming insolvent or bankrupt; the failure of bank.
7. A person or thing that proves unsuccessful.

In the media, we hear about failing teachers, failing students and schools. Students who get retained, say they failed a grade, as much as the educators around them try to call it something else. There are so many ways we fail. Some of those failures are socially accepted and others are not.

If someone fails a test, they are encouraged to move on and try again. If they fail to get into the college of their choice they are persuaded to find another one that would be more fitting. When someone fails to make the basketball team or the lead part in a play they eventually brush themselves off and try again but for a while they feel like a failure. The feel like no one around them had ever failed before and they are the only ones who met such a cruel fate. However, those are all socially acceptable way to fail. We have all encountered those issues from time to time.

Other times, failure is not acceptable. When leaders or politicians make grave mistakes and lie to the public, they fail to gain or maintain public trust. When adults action, put them and others in harm's way they fail to understand the magnitude of their situations. Others blindly keep failing never to learn from their mistakes.

Too many people, the opposite of retention is social promotion. Educators are as tired of social promotion as they are of retention. Social promotion is indeed just as harmful as retention. A child should never get to fifth or sixth grade without learning to read. If that happens, the adults {parents, educators, administrators} around those students have failed to help those children.

Sometimes people talk about failure as if it is a good thing. Other times people talk about failure as if kids should have to wear a badge on their arm to signify that they have failed. The truth is that not every one succeeds. I would venture to guess that everyone fails from time to time; it's just that not everyone wants to talk about their failures.

Failure comes in many forms. When a child fails, it is an opportunity for them to learn from their mistakes or how to make something better. When we treat a child like a failure, after they make mistake, then we have failed at our job as adults because we did not show them compassion. If a child is made to feel like a failure rather than educated on the on the benefits of failure, they may never be able to succeed in life.

This is fatherly love who did not withhold His only begotten Son against our redemption

But rather gave him out as a ransom to pay our sins and redeem us from our failing state. Adam and Eve were tested in the book of Genesis by God who made them governors over everything He had created {Genesis 2:15-16}. Unfortunately, they blew this golden opportunity sinning against God which automatically rendered the entire human race on earth failure, "for all have sinned and fall short of the glory of God" {Romans 3:23}. And for God to show us that beautiful compassion and mentoring love once again He gave us His Son to atone our sins on the cross, and He is asking us to "arise and "shine". Many Christians fail to address the issue of failure by working vigorously on its causes and we channel everything to the Devil which is wrong.

We should not forget the fact that success comes through rapidly fixing our mistakes, rather than getting things right first time. At this point, let us look at some few causes to know how to deal with failure.

CAUSES OF FAILURE

Have you ever been so afraid of failing at something that you decided not to try it at all?

Or has a fear of failure, meant that, subconsciously, you undermined your own efforts to avoid the possibility of a larger failure? Many of us have probably experienced this at one time or another. The fear of failing can be immobilizing—it can cause us to do nothing, and therefore resist us to moving forward. And when we allow fear to stop our forward progress in life, we are likely to miss some great opportunities along the way. The following are some of the causes we need to look at if we really want to be successful in life.

1. LACK OF A SPECIFIC PURPOSE IN LIFE:-

This is one of the biggest problems facing many leaders in the world including church leaders. You cannot hope to succeed in any field of life you don't have a central purpose. If you don't have a definite goal in your life then you will jump from one activity to another with no success. Almost 97% of people think and act in this way. That is why successful people, who have a clear goal in their life, are very few.

Many Christians suffer from this. They have been brainwashed to believe that prayer and faith are the only two things you need as a Christian to succeed in life but I here to tell to suggest to you that such a doctrine is a mere fantasy. You already have Christ who is shinning in you, therefore, your part to play to become a successful Christian is to have a definite goal or purpose. Stop being jack of all trade and stick to one thing that you believe in your heart will help you to become successful. Many believers today behave as if they don't know what they have and that they want in life. Stop changing jobs and careers and pursue one thing at a time.

2. LACK OF EDUCATION:-

The prophet Hosea said; "My people are destroyed for lack of knowledge: because you have rejected knowledge—" {Hosea 4:6}, "Therefore my people are gone into captivity, because they have no knowledge; and their honorable men are famished—" {Isaiah 5:13}

Most of the successful people are "self-educated" or self-made" as individuals. You can have five college degrees but if you don't apply the knowledge it's a waste. What counts is the applied knowledge with a plan of action and not just knowledge. One of the effects of lack of knowledge is that the people become ignorant of their goals in life which sometimes renders most graduates jobless on our streets.

3. LACK OF SELF DISCIPLINE:-

Discipline means self-control. You must control yourself and decrease your negative habits and qualities. If you don't conquer yourself, it will conquer you. A person who is rich, or who has financial problem, or who simply knows what their goals are also must have the discipline to maintain a personal life. A disciplined business person should bring that same discipline to their relationships with friends and family and community, knowing that real success is not possible with money alone. If it was, we would not see horror stories about lottery winners flaming out after winning the lottery. We have heard thousands of stories about mega million and power ball winners who are now homeless as a result of lack of discipline towards the riches. As you pray to the Lord to grant you success, try as much as you can to discipline yourself by sticking to your values. Remember discipline is the key to success. "For the flesh lusts against the Spirit, and the Spirit against the flesh; and these are contrary the one to the; another; so that you cannot do the things that you would" {Galatians 5:17}.

4. PROCRASTINATION

It is one of the major causes of failure. These kind of people are waiting for opportunities come to them instead of seeking for the opportunities. They think that someday the time the time will be right to act. That "right" time never comes. The Bible shows us "the sluggard". The sluggard is a character who lives a world of procrastination. His thoughts outweigh his actions. The sluggard is foolishly unaware of consequences.

"Go to the ant, you sluggard; consider his ways and be wise! It has no commander, no overseer or ruler. it stores its provisions in summer and gathers its food at harvest. How long will you lie there, you sluggard? When will you get up from your slumber? A little sleep, a little slumber, a little folding of the hands to rest-poverty will come on you like a bandit and scarcity like an armed man" {proverbs 6:6-12}.

5. LACK OF PERSISTENCE

This is another killer to many dreams. Most people are good starters but they stop in the run when the first obstacle comes. Obstacles are a chance to become better. They are ways to use your mind and improve yourself. Quitters cannot hope to succeed, of any kind. Bear in mind that winners never quit and quitters never win anything meaningful in their lives. Fight the good fight to the end and you will surely eat the fruit of your labor, which is the goodness of the land the Lord your God has promised His children. "I have fought a good fight, I have finished my course, I have kept the faith, henceforth there is laid up for me a crown of righteousness, which the Lord the righteous judge, shall give me at that day; and not to me only, but unto all them also that love his appearing" {11 Timothy 4:5-8}.

6. BEING NEGATIVE

If you are a negative, then your whole world is negative. Your subconscious mind tells you that you can not do it. Your subconscious mind commands your conscious self that you "really" can't do it. Apostle Paul said; I can do all things through Christ who strengthen me" {Philippians 4:13}. Of the strength which Christ can impart, Paul had had abundant experience; and now his whole reliance was there. It was not any native ability which he had; not in any vigor of body or of mind; not in any power which there was in his own resolutions; it was the strength which he derived from the redeemer. By that he was enable to bear cold, and hunger; by that, he met temptations and persecutions; and by that, he engaged in the performance of his arduous duties. Here, we see Paul to be a positive thinker, he did not allow the negative aspect of his journey deter him.

7. REFUSING TO TAKE A RISK

If you are extremely careful and take no risks then you can't expect to make the difference. There are many opportunities out there for you to grab but they come with a price. Being over cautious limit you to mediocrity and eventually, lead you to failure. Remember, it is risky not to take a risk. Many Business men and women fail because they are afraid to take a risk by trying new ideas. Many people also fail in their career because they are afraid of the price they have to pay. "He that love father or mother more than me is not worthy of me; and he that loves a son or a daughter more than me is not worthy of me, And he that takes not his cross, and follows me; is not worthy of me. He that finds his life shall lose it: and he that loses his life for my sake shall find it." {Matthew 10:37-39}.

8. WRONG SELECTION OF ASSOCIATES

This is very critical. We cannot do everything by ourselves. The colleagues we work with are a capital for our business. Successful and intelligent partners are one of the keys for our own success. Work with people who are blessed with the skill and knowledge in the area of your business or career and that will help you to become successful in life. "Do not be deceived, bad company destroys a good character" {1 Corinthians 15:33}. The bible goes on to suggest that "He who walks with wise men will be wise, but the companion of fools will be destroyed, "Proverb 13:20}. "Don't spend time with those who are foolish or eventually you won't be able to discern knowledge" {Proverb14:7}. If you are in the company of those who are wise, you will gain wisdom. If you are in the company of those who are evil, you too will become evil, therefore, choose the wise and you will succeed in your life span.

9. DIVIDE YOUR ACTIONS

This is a typical mistake. Spreading your energy and efforts on multiple causes and not concentrating on one cause. Sooner or later you will realize that you will not succeed to any of them. Many people always try to become jack of all trade and they end up achieving nothing in life. Stick to one particular and definite cause and pursue it to the end with all your energy and effort with good people, "No servant can serve two masters, for either he will hate the one and love the other, or he will be devoted to the one and despise the other", {Luke 16:13}.

10. LACK OF HONESTY

This is the master key of success. Without honesty, your credibility will vanish in no time and you cannot hope to expand and of course retain your business. People are not as stupid as you think. They can understand the fake, may be not immediately but in the long turn they will go away and spread around the world the negative messages about you. "Lying lips are an abomination to the Lord, but those who act faithfully are his delight." {Proverb 12:22}. "Better is the poor person who walk in his integrity than one who is crooked in speech and is a fool" {Proverb 19:1}.

HOW TO OVERCOME FAILURE

When it comes to failing, our egos are our own worst enemies. As soon as things start going wrong, our defense mechanism kick in. tempting us to do what we can to save face. Yet these very normal reactions,— denial, chasing your losses, and hedonic editing wreak havoc on our ability to adapt. We should also understand that challenge motivates people. JFK famously said they were going to the moon not because it was easy, but because it was hard. Google Larry Page even went so far as to say: "If you are not doing some things that are crazy, then you are doing wrong things."

It is impossible to live your life and not face failure. Many at times we get so caught in the failure that we lose all power to overcome it. This is why it is very important that you learn how to overcome failure.

1. UNDERSTAND THAT THE ONLY PATH TO SUCCESS IS THROUGH FAILURE

Keep a positive perspective and understand that you only failed because you tried, had you not tried then you wouldn't have failed and then you wouldn't have succeeded either. It is like a fork on the road, one or the other; you have to cross failure to overcome failure. Let us look at the following people who tasted failure, yet became successful.

HENRY FORD: while Ford is today known for his innovative assembly line and America-made cars, he was not an instant success. In fact, his early businesses failed and left him broke five times before he founded the successful Ford Motor Company.

THOMAS EDISON: In his early years, teachers told Edison was "too stupid to learn anything." Work was no better, as he was fired from his first two jobs for not being productive enough. Even as an inventor, Edison made 1,000 unsuccessful attempts at inventing the light bulb. Of course, all those unsuccessful attempts finally resulted in the design that worked.

ISSAC NEWTON: Newton was undoubtedly a genius when it came to math, but he had some failings early on. He never did particularly well in school and when put him in charge of running the family farm, he failed miserably, so poorly in fact that an uncle took charge and sent him off to Cambridge where he finally blossomed into the scholar we know today.

They did not see failure as the end of the journey but a path to success. The bible makes it clear that; "For a righteous man shall fall seven times and rise again" {Proverb 24:16}.

2. REMAIN CALM AND REFLECT

Think about it no matter what you do now, nothing will change the past. Don't channel your frustration and anger in a negative way.

Keep your composure and channel your emotions and your feelings to motivate you to try again. Failures allow their emotions to push them to hang their fighting boots on the wall but winners see it to be a driven force to catapult them to the next level. "And the peace of God, which transcends all understanding, will guard your hearts and minds in Christ Jesus." {Philippians 4:7}.

3. LEARN FROM YOUR FAILURES

Very often people don't pay attention to their failures in way to cope with them, when actually the time you learn the most is when you try and fail. If you can learn the mistakes you made, maybe, next time you can overcome failures and reach success. Try to learn from your mistakes and pick up the broken pieces and begin to mend them together once again.

4. DON'T GIVE UP OR RATIONALIZE YOUR FAILURE

Many times when you fail to rationalize it, you give yourself a reason to give up. For example, a fox in the woods, he sees some grapes and jumps to get them, after a couple of failed attempts, the fox gives up and says to rationalize his failure that they were probably sour anyway. Keep fighting and never think of quitting.

5. SELF CONFIDENCE

Never let failures even scratch your confidence level. If you fail it does not mean you can never do it. Keep going at it and believe in yourself, because it's greatest key in overcoming failure. Talk to yourself in front of your mirror at least once a day to encourage yourself. Never look down yourself and don't allow the past failings seen on your face. Raise your confidence level and tell yourself that you can try again.

6. STAYING THE PRESENT

Don't wander in the past but rather concentrate in what you are doing "now". By staying in the present you allow yourself to grow from your failure and overcome it rather than drowning in your own pain. Use your past as a stepping stone to correct your present to get a beautiful failure.

CHAPTER 3

THE LIGHT DOESN'T COMPROMISE WITH SIN

INTRODUCTION

We live in a culture where the concept of sin has become and entangled with the legalistic argument over right or wrong. When many of us consider "What is sin", we think of violations of the Ten Commandments. Even then, we tend to think of murder and adultery as a "major" sins compared to lying, cursing or idolatry.

The truth is that, sin, as defined in the original translations of the bible, means "to miss the mark." The mark in this case, is the standard of perfection established by God and evidenced by Jesus Christ. Viewed in that light, it is clear that we are all sinners.

The Apostle Paul says in Romans 3:23, "All have sinned and fall short of the glory of God." In light of this, it does no good to compare ourselves to others. We cannot escape our failure to be righteous in our own strength. This is by God's design, because only when we understand our weakness, we will consider relying on the atoning sacrifice of Jesus Christ.

WHAT IS SIN—A BLIBLICAL PERSPECTIVE

Sin is mentioned hundreds of times in the bible, starting with the "original" sin when Adam and Eve ate of the tree of knowledge. Often it seems as sin is simply the violation of any of God's law's, including the Ten Commandments.

Paul, however put this in perspective in Romans 3:20, when he says, "therefore no one will be declared righteous in His sight by observing the law, rather, through the law we become conscious of sin."

God wanted us to recognize out sins. Even those who have not committed murdering or adultery will find themselves convicted of being lying, or of worshipping false idols like wealth or power ahead of God. Tragically, sin in any amount will distance us from God.

"Surely, the arm of the Lord is not too short to save, nor His ear too dull to hear," says Isaiah 59:1-2. "But your iniquities have separated you from your God; your sins have hidden His face from you, so that He will not hear."

We must resist the temptation to act as if we are righteous, especially by leaning on our good works.

"if we claim to be righteous without sin, we deceive ourselves and the truth is not in us, if we confess our sins, he is faithful and just to forgive our sins, and purify us from all unrighteousness. If we claim we have not sinned, we make him out to be a liar, and his word is not in us." {1John1:8-10}.

THE DOCTRINE OF SIN

1. MAN WAS CREATED WITH FREEDOM OF CHOICE

The question many contemporary people ask is; if God really created a perfect world, then how did sin originated? As we noted earlier, man was originally created in God's image. This included in the fact that he was a rational creature with the freedom of choice. Man was originally in a condition of true holiness, which allowed him unhindered access to God and a propensity to choose that which was good. But for such a freedom to be truly "free" meant that man was also given the choice to disobey and do evil. The same moral freedom that enabled man to choose to serve God also enabled him to choose to serve himself. Why didn't God just create man without the ability to sin?

Then they could enjoy the unbroken communion with God forever. To do that would miss the point of man being God's image, which includes the freedom to willingly love and serve God. Man would have simply been robots, and that's no kind of love relationship, and it does not approve man being the image of God. We can program our computers to work, and do all the right things, and even "talk," but that does not mean that we have meaningful relationships with them. God knew what would happen and still thought it was worth the risk.

2. MAN CHOOSE TO ABUSE HIS FREEDOM AND SIN

Man was created to enjoy total freedom. He was created to be a free agent and sinless in nature. Let us consider the following:

*The biblical account of the fall is found in Gen. 3.
*Serpent tempted Adam and Eve to sin {3:15}.
*They knew the rules, yet they gave in to the desire-the pleasure to be obtained from eating the fruit.
*Adam and Eve made a choice to abuse their freedom.
*They choose to yield to desire and eat the forbidden fruit.
*I am convinced that this fruit must have been Durian!.
*Sin came about as the result of the abuse of this freedom.
*Neither God or Satan "created" evil, since evil is not a thing of substance which can be created.

*Rather, evil is a relationship that is entered into by those who freely choose to oppose the righteous command of God and choose instead to follow their own ways.

THE IMMEDIATE RESULT OF SIN ADAM AND EVE {3:7-10}

a. They learned the difference between the good and evil

* They recognized their sin and they felt shame and guilt.
* For the first time they felt shame at their nakedness.
* They sewed fig leaves together and made coverings for themselves.
* Yes, they knew no more, but they did not like it.

b. They had broken fellowship with God.

* Sin has separated them from God, {spiritual death}.
* In their guilt, they tried to hide from God when He came to them.
* Principle; Spiritual guilt separates us from God.

c. They were punished for their sin {3:14-24}.

* The serpent was cursed above all animals.
* When he crawls on his belly, he will eat dust-all his life.
* There will be enmity between man and the serpent.
* He will ultimately be destroyed by the seed of the woman.
* Eve was cursed with pain in childbirth.
* Her desire should be her husband.
* Adam must work hard to survive.
* He will have hindrances in his work and will face physical death.
* Adam and Eve have to leave the garden.
* Therefore life in the world as we know it {the real world} begins.

THE ULTIMATE CONSEQUENCES OF
THE SINS OF ADAM AND EVE

a. Universal depravity of mankind

*   Through Adam, sin entered the entire human race.
*   Some questions why Scripture places blame on Adam, when Eve was the first to give in? As a matter of fact man was made to be the head of everything including Eve.
*   God had given prohibition to Adam, before Eve was created.
*   In making her decision, Eve had two sets of data to choose from: one report from Adam, and one report from Satan.
*   Eve rejected Adam's information to follow Satan.
*   In making his decisions, Adam also had two sets of data: God's and Satan's. Adam rejected God to follow Satan.
*   So the New Testament teaches us that because of Adam's sin we too are all sinners.
*   Rom. 5:12-19; "sin to all from one man—.
*   Adam as the head of the race, sinned, in a legal and representative sense.
*   When Adam sinned, he was acting in this representative capacity and as a result all humans share in the legal responsibility of that sin and now have a corrupted and depraved nature.
*   ANALOGY; our president/ prime minister acts as a representative on behalf of the people.
*   Our legal head/ representative acts on our behalf, and his actions will be reckoned to us.
*   In the same way, in God's eyes, man is guilty; he has violated God's intention for mankind, and is liable to punishment.
*   Some would argue that all people are not equally bad.
*   There are some non-saved people who are pretty "good" {nice}.
*   ILLUSTRATION; Place three people according to their goodness.
*   The peak of Mount Everest 29 000 feet.
*   From our human perspective, they may look different.

* But from God's high standard/ position {the moon}, it all looks the same.
* Equally separated from God—all men are equally lost.

b. Loss of communion and open fellowship with God

* Before the fall Adam and Eve had a very natural communion with God.
* But sin resulted in a separation between God and man.
* There is now a barrier that separates man from God.
* Man is unable to come back into relationship with God w/o assistance.

THE NATURE OF SIN

* Having noted the entrance of sin into the world, we must now examine it more closely.
* We have implied that sin, most basically, is selfishness-wanting to fulfill one's desires, no matter the cost.
* What is the nature of this "sin" against which we fight?
* Most simply put, sin {hamartia} means missing the mark.
* To deviate from the correct way—it is actually used of a sling missing the mark {Judges 20:16}.
* While this may sound at first it is referring to just accidental "poor aim."
* The word implies that a wicked man misses the right mark because he deliberately aims toward the wrong one.
* Hamartia denotes deliberate action—one misses the mark because he has intentionally, aimed at the wrong target {Roman 6:1-2}.
* Sin is a lack of conformity to the moral law of God, either in act, disposition, or state.

THE CHARACTER OF SIN

a. Sin is an inward inclination that results in outward acts.

* Some think of sin as doing evil acts.
* But sin is an inherent inward disposition inclining us to do wrong

MAN MUST DEAL WITH SIN IN HIS LIFE IN TWO DIFRRENT WAYS

{1} Sin Is A State Of Existence: Original Sin

* "Original Sin" denotes the sinful state into which we are born.
* Show Comic: Nursery; class, today's topic is original sin—

WE ARE BORN WITH A SINFUL NATURE

* Because of Adam, we are all born into original sin.
* Roman 5:12, "sin entered the world through one man" See also Roman 5:14-19, Gen. 6:5
* All people are actually born with a sinful nature, so we were sinners before we even sinned.
* We sin because we are sinners
* Not because we sin, we are sinners
* See Ps. 51:5; Eph. 2:3; Job 14:4; John 3:16, etc.
* Rom. 5:19; 7:14, 8:4-8, Gal. 5:17

The Sinful State Is Sometimes Called Total Depravity

* Man is born a hopeless sinner
* The corruption of sin extends to every part of our nature
* See Rom. 7:18, 8:7; Eph. 4:18, 2 Tim. 3:2-4
* Total depravity does not mean that we have no inmate knowledge of God or conscious left.

* But it does mean that we are unable to change on our own, or make ourselves right.
* We dox not have the ability to on our own to restore ourselves the right relationship with God.
* We cannot do acts which make us worthy of God's acceptance.
* See Jn. 3:3, 6:44; 1 Cor. 2:14, Eph. 2:1
* I think it is pretty obvious that we are all born sinners
* All you have to do is look around you to see that
* So, not only is sin a state of existence {original sin} but—

{2} Sin Involves Specific Acts: Actual Sin

* Those sin which we can and do personally commit
* Because we are guilty of original sin, we will do actual sin
* We all commit actual sin because we are sinners

Actual Sin Can Take One OF Two Forms:

{A} SINS OF COMMISSION

* Doing things that should not be done
* Some sins are explicitly specified in the bible, some are implicitly specified
* It is interesting but the closer we grow to God, the more aware we are of sin
* When we are new Christians, it's just the major sins
* But as we become more like Him, we realize all the areas in which we fall so short.
* Show Comic; putting and end to sin is like trying to—
* In addition, to sins of commission, there are . . . .

{B SINS OF OMISSION

* It is just as much sin not to do things that we should be done
* One little boy obviously did not understand this word

* When the teacher asked the class, "what are the sins of omission?" he quickly responded
* "Those are the sins we should have committed but we did not"
* The bible tells us that to know what to do, and do not do it, is a sin
* James tells us that we should not only be hearers of the word but doers

SIN ENTAILS SPIRITUAL DISABILITY

* Sin alters our inner condition—our character
* Just as cracked mirror reflects a distorted picture, so as the image of God in us had been distorted and disturbed
* There is a separation from God {Ps. 51}
* Only through a renewal of the mind can the individual be restored to an undistorted, spiritually healthy condition {Roman 12:2}}

SIN IS INCOMPLETE FULFILMENT OF GOD'S STANDARD

* It is failure not to keep God's commands and standard of righteousness
* We may do this simply by falling short of His expectations, or by actually breaking his law and doing the opposite of what he requires
* In Romans 7, Paul tells us that this is a daily struggle for Christians
* We want to do what is right, but that old human nature gets in the way

SIN IS DISPLACEMENT OF GOD

* Placing something else, anything else, in the supreme place which belongs to God is sin

* This can even be placing our own selfish desires before God's will
* This bowls down to a love of self-becoming magnified and one begins to a place of self-interest above those of God—This is what leads to sin
* Simply put, sin leads from being self-centered rather than being a centered self, whose true source of motivation is God

CONSEQUENCES OF SIN

* Because God is just, righteous and holy, sin is abhorrent to God
* Therefore, God must ultimately punish sin

PUNISHMENT

a. Definition of punishment

* The infliction of pain or suffering because of some misdeed
* Misdeed—sin
* The one to inflict pain / suffering—God
* Because of man's sinful conditions, he is liable to God's punishment

PUNISHMENT MAY BE TO REFORM THE SINNER

* God punishes us to reform us
* While God's judgment does have a retributive character {punishment they deserve}, it also has a restorative goal
* "The Lord disciplines those whom he loves, and chastises every son whom he receives"
  {Heb. 12:6}
* Sometimes God disciplines us for the sake of helping us to see the error of our ways and turning from them {Ps. 107:10-16}

PUNISHMENT FOR THE SATISFACTION OF DIVINE JUSTICE

Achan, Ananias and Saphira were punished by a just God, and a just God must maintain his holiness. God's justice was called into question, and must be vindicated. This is not always done immediately and instantaneously {thank God}. Key: in the satisfaction of God's justice, deterring and reforming can take place, but the bottom line is his holy nature. Physical death and eternal condemnation await sinners

CHAPTER 4

THE ENEMY OF GOD'S "SHINNING LIGHT"

INTRODUCTION

The history of Satan began with riches and honor. Satan had a glorious future. He then became jealous and proud. He refused to repent and his future became dark. The events of history continue as Satan comes to earth and tries to become the god of this world. world. He delights in destruction. Satan would like to destroy every person on the planet and to lead them to hell which is his abode. As you read the history of Satan, know that Jesus is the winner man whereas Satan is the looser with all his cohorts. It is my concern and prayer to God my savior that you will wake up from your slumber and take up with you the whole armor of God and walk uprightly in the kingdom of light.

The battle of manipulation against the people of God is intensifying daily. The children of light therefore have to step into the authority which belongs to us, in order to be over comers against the wiles of the devil. Our ignorance has paved way for Satan to destroy our glory for too long.

WHO REALLY IS SATAN

You cannot know somebody who the person really is unless you have knowledge about the person. You are therefore going to know who the god of this world {Satan} is, the destroyer of the creation of God. This entity was called Lucifer. He was given full wisdom above all archangels and the angels in heaven. He was perfect in his ways from the day that he was created till iniquity was created till iniquity was found in him m,{Ezekiel 28:15}.

Satan is an entity with wisdom and the only archangel who was having two positions when he was in heaven. He performed the position of archangel, and the same time cherub. Not only cherub, but anointed with perfection {Ezekiel 28:14}. From the standpoint of his positions as wise, high hierarchy of angel, anointed and at the same time perfect in his ways. It depicts that God endowed in him great things which made him outstanding in heaven among the archangels and the entire angels.

Many Christians think they can overcome Satan in their sinful state of life. Whoever commits sin is of the devil, {1Jn 3:8}. There is an indication that you are his servant. "And a servant is not greater than his master" {Jn. 13:16}.

All that Satan need from you is to fight you to the end to loose the glory which enables you to shine in your Father's kingdom of light. The easiest way to deal with this is to cause you to sin.

SATAN AGAINST THE GLORY

When we were in the world, thus in the clutches of the devil, he knew our fall shorts; it then becomes his weapon to war against us. Once upon a time, we were slaves to Satan when we did not know the Lord. It therefore plunged us into the hands of the devil as salves, {Rom. 6:16}. The moment the Lord delivers and join you into his kingdom, the evil one will assign unto you a demon to track and defeat your walk with God. That familiar spirit is the one, who will handle your information to their high hierarchy for your destruction, if he incapable to handle you.

All what the devil is seeking from you the child of light is to destroy the light which the Lord has bestowed in your life. The only way the Satan can do this is to destroy the hedge which the Great God has bestowed on your life.

THE HEDGE

"And now go to, I will tell you what I will do to my vineyard: I will take away the hedge thereof, and it shall be eaten up; and break down the wall thereof, and it shall be trodden down" {Isaiah 5:5}.

Every child of God's life is hidden with Christ in God, {Colossians 3:3}. That is the only ultimate protection a child of God will ever had in the kingdom of God. Nobody can touch you without defeating Jesus, and further it up to reach God the Father. But hey! The Lord of Glory has already defeated the devil over 2000 years ago so who is he that can touch you? No one else! The devil is fully aware of this, therefore he has orchestrated means to destroy what the good Lord has used for the protection of his people that is what we called "HEDGE".

The very moment you come to the Lord, the Holy Spirit seals you into the kingdom of his dear Son, {Eph. 1:13}, and the Great Father God will hedge you against any manipulation of Satan and his forces of darkness. When it is done, beloved, no demon from the pit of hell can penetrate into it for destruction. You then become more secured evermore in your daily Christian walk with God. In this phase, instead of the devil being an enemy to your walk with God, you can be an enemy to yourself if you give place to the devil, {Eph. 4:27}. The only thing can allow the devil to destroy this protective measure is when you permit him to do so.

Ask yourself, why many men of God fell from grace to grace? They were defeated by the same tactic by Satan. Do you really believe that an anointed man of God who paid a great price will intentionally sell his anointing for just a common sex? Nevertheless! The moment you become God shinning star, you are marked as an enemy in the kingdom of darkness. Satan then will assign unto you his powerful agents to track you and cause you to backslide. If you are able to resist all the attempts of the demonic powers, they will send "sin" into your door. That is why Jesus cautioned us to pray that we should not fall into temptations, {Mark 14:38}.

The major supernatural force, the devil uses to overcome the people of God is "sin," which is the sting of death. Sin is the sole element on earth that subject one under the forces of darkness. The moment you transgress the law of God, the protection measures the Lord has placed in your life is broken. This leads you to be meat or prey to any being in the dark world. Every wind or storm will just blow in your life and circumstances will bound you up.

In this stage of life, there is a way out to put things together to find your self again in the canopy of the Lord. The faithful God will never leave you or forsake you only if you will put on your garment of righteousness and seek the face of the Lord.

As it has been treated in chapter three, every detail has been provided to help you to deal with "sin" which is the ultimate goal of the devil to deter you from becoming the shinning light of the Most High God of the universe.

HOW TO PROTECT YOUR SHINNING LIGHT

Beloved, many Christians think Satan is easy to overcome by oneself. No! It is a wrong notion, because our might is beneath his strength. It was through our Savior who defeated him and put him to naught, {Colossians 2:15}. Because of his love towards us, he delegated his authority unto us. Without the cross, everyone on this planet would be a captive to Satan and all the beings in the dark world.

To be a shinning light in the Lord and to enjoy all the treasures in heaven on earth, you need to be strong in the Lord and let the word of God abide in you, {1Jn. 2:14}. The book of Ephesians has given us all the details of how to overcome the enemy and destroy his strongholds, {Ephesians 6:10-18}.

A Christian who can enter into the dark world and shut the enemy off is the one who is strong in the Lord and is clothed with the power of his might. You might ask yourself, who is this kind of Christian? Is it the one who attend the church every service, or the one who is the leader of the church? Or the one who believe the triune God? Far from that perspective, for it is the one who knows the word of God, and possess the unction of the Holy Spirit, {the one whom Christ is manifested in his body}. To achieve this, you need to develop your spiritual man in order to be fervent in the Spirit.

HOW TO DEVELOP YOUR SPIRIT AGAINST THE DEVIL

* Study the word of God—consume the word and let the word also consume you
* Be baptized in the Holy Spirit and pray in the Spirit, {Eph. 6:18}
* Humility {1Peter 5:6}
* Obedience to the word of God {John. 14:15}
* Be the epistle of the word of God
* Obedient to the voice of the Spirit
* Prayer and fasting
* Walk in love

When the inner man is developed, the Holy Spirit will empower you to stand fast in the liberty which Christ has made you free, {Gal. 5:1}. Then you will start walking in the Spirit which will demonstrate the fruit of the Spirit in your Christian daily walk with God, {Gal. 5:22}.

At this point in time, you have been changed from glory to glory and become Christ like. Therefore, your shinning star "glory" will shatter the demonic activities against your life. And instead of being manipulated, it is rather you who will deal with the forces of darkness and direct them what to do. You would have every authority and power to deal with them as the Spirit leads you. The moment your light start burning, you will be a great enemy to the forces of darkness, but take heart, you have overcome the world because of the brilliant light, which is the glory of God in your life.

VARIIOUS NAMES OF SATAN

The Bible calls Satan by many different names. Each name has a slightly different meaning. The many other names for Satan give a fuller picture of who Satan is and what he does. There are more names of Satan in the Bible than for anyone else except Jesus Christ.

Abaddon:—Hebrew name for Satan meaning "Destruction" {Rev. 9:11}

Accuser:—Rev. 12:10

Adversary:—1Peter 5:8

Angel of Light:—2Cor 11:14

Angel of the bottomless pit:—Rev 9:11

Anointed Covering Cherub:—Ezek 28:14

Antichrist:—1Jn 4:3

Apollyon:—Greek name for Satan meaning "Destroyer" Rev. 9:11

Beast:—Rev 14:9-10

Beelzebub: Mat 12:24

Belial:—2Cor 6:15

Deceiver:—Rev 12:9

Devil:—1Jn 3:8

Dragon:—Rev 12:9

Enemy:—Mat 13:39

Evil one:—Jn 17:15

Father of lies:—Jn 8:44

God of this age:—2Cor 4:4

King of Babylon:—Isaiah 14:4

King of Tyre:—Ezek 28:12

Lawless one:—2Thess 2:8-10

Leviathan:—Isaiah 27:1

Liar:—Jn 8:44

Little horn:—Daniel 8:9-11

Lucifer:—Isaiah 14:12-14

Man of sin:—2Thess 2:3-4

Murderer:—Jn 8:44

Power of darkness:—Col 1:13-14

Prince of the power of the air: Eph 2:1-2

Roaring lion:—1Peter 5:8

Rulers of the darkness:—Eph 6:12

Ruler of demons:—Lk 11:15

Ruler of this world:—Jn 12:31-32

Satan:—Mk 1:13

Serpent of old:—Rev 12:9

Son of perdition:—2Thess 2:3-4

Star:—Rev 9:1

Tempter:—Mat 4:3

Thief:—Jn 10:10

Wicked one:—Eph 6:16

CHAPTER 5

PRAYER AND FASTING

INTRODUCTION

The topic "prayer and fasting" has won a huge global attention because people have mixed feelings about it. Many people think that it is a waste of time and a sheer madness to starve yourself and pray for days to a certain supreme deity who even does not exist, while Christians and other groups on the other hand also believe that as human beings as we are, we cannot do without prayer. Prayer is the practice of the presence of God. Prayer is the only channel through which we can communicate with God. Therefore it is the place where pride is abandoned, hope is lifted, and supplication is made. Prayer is the place of admitting our need, of adopting humility, and claiming dependence upon God. Prayer is the needful practice of the Christians. Prayer is the exercise of faith and hope. It is the privilege of touching the heart of the God the Father through the Son of God, Jesus Christ our Lord.

The bible speaks much of prayer. But, sometimes, too often, we ignore prayer and seek to accomplish in the strength of our own wills, the things that we desire to have or happen. For those of us who are too often guilty of this, we need to bow our knees, confess our sins, receive God's forgiveness, and plead that the will of the Lord be done above in our lives. God is sovereign, and loving, and He knows the best for us, and others, even if it does not always seem to make the most sense for us.

We often come to the Lord with legitimate requests for healing, conversions, and needs but yet, the answers we hope for often are not answered. We wonder and sometimes doubt. Yet, we persevere and praise God. We pray because we know that God hears us and we desire to also to see results. We should pray consistently and by faith, trusting God for answering our prayers. We should intercede for others trusting God touching their needs. We should pray and when our prayers are answered or not remember this; If we knew what the Lord knew, we would not change a thing.

Prayer changes the one praying because in prayer, you are in the presence of the Most High Creator of the universe as you lay before Him denying yourself complete in confession and dependence. There is nothing to hide when are in quiet supplication, reaching into the deepest part of ourselves, and admitting our needs and failures. In so doing, our hearts are comforted and pride is stripped and we enjoy the presence of God. James 4:8 says, "Draw near to God and He will draw near to you."

There is another benefit of prayer; peace. "Be anxious for nothing, but in everything by prayer and supplication with thanksgiving let your request be made known to God. And the peace of God which passes all understanding will, guard your hearts and your minds in Christ Jesus." {Phil. 4:6-7}.

I suppose that we can test our prayer life and dependence upon God by the peace or not in our hearts. In all things, we are to seek the Lord and in His continued presence. Peace will surely be our gain when we sincerely pray.

WHY DO WE PRAY?

A friend of mine one day asked me this interesting question. I told him we have uncountable reasons which will compel us to pray as Christians. Let us discuss the following.

1. God has always demands his people to pray, "Pray always" {1Thess. 5:17}.
2. Jesus prayed, sometimes all night long, and He is our model—we do what He did.
3. The tradition of prayer has been a cornerstone of the faith through history.
4. God's people named throughout in the bible were always praying.
5. Prayer ushers to the presence of God.
6. Prayer reins in our overactive, worry-prone control-oriented minds.
7. We remind ourselves of Jesus' Lordship as we pray. It helps us not be presumptuous.
8. We align ourselves with the Spirit, allowing Him to counsel us.
9. We learn to recognize Jesus voice as we pray, "my sheep hears my voice" {Jn. 10:27}.
10. We bring our petitions to God and He answers them. {2Thess.1:11}.
11. God deserves our praise. We glorify Him as we pray, {1Thess. 1:12}.
12. The whole bible is the product of prayer—God revealing stuff to holy men of God, giving to humanity by writings.
13. The early disciples prayed all the time, and even after the ascension of Christ. I hope this will help you increase your prayer ability to excel in the communion with the Great God the Father.

WHEN DO WE PRAY?

Do we even have a specific time to pray, or does it really matter when we pray? I think the following will help us as Christians to know the specific times our Lord Jesus Christ instructed us to communicate our prayers to the Father.

WHEN WE ARE SAD:—Dark hours come to all of us, whether through sickness, death, marital conflict, conflict with children, loneliness, or whatever. When our hearts are heavy, we should lift them up in prayer to God. Don't forget to pray.

WHEN WE ARE HAPPY:—Few of us forget to pray during adversity, moreover, many of us are like the nine lepers whom Jesus healed. They forgot to return and thank him for his blessings. When things are going well in life, we should praise God for answered prayers and his guidance in our lives.

WHEN WE ARE TEMPTED:—None of us are so perfect that we are not tempted to sin. The desires of the flesh reside in our body and through them Satan tempts us. When sore temptations come to us, we should pause to pray. Jesus taught us to pray that we enter not into temptations. When He taught his disciples to pray, he said, "And lead us not temptations, but deliver us from evil", {Matt. 6:13}. Not only will the Lord lead us from temptations, he also has promised to help us with the way of escape when the temptations come upon us. Paul wrote, "There has no temptation taken you but such as is common to man, but God is faithful, who will not suffer you to be tempted above that you are able; but will with the temptation also make a way to escape, that you may be able to bear it" {1Cor. 10:13}.

WHEN WE ARE WORRIED:—Christians have been taught to cast their burden on the Lord. Paul wrote, in Phil. 4:16, "Be careful for nothing; but in everything by prayer and supplication with thanksgiving let your request be known unto God". When we are worried about a problem, let us pause and analyze and evaluate the situation. If there is something we can do to solve the problem, let's be busy doing it. If there is nothing we can do to solve the problem, let us lay it before God in prayer and be ready to accept whatever his providence gives to us in answer to that prayer. Someone has said that worry is like a rocking chair—you move a lot, but you don't go anywhere. Rather than allowing worrying and fretting about the possible problems we may face tomorrow to ruin today, let us live today to its fullest and cast our burdens on the Lord.

WHEN WE HAVE A PROBLEM TO SOLVE:—The day before Jesus chose his twelve disciples, he spent the entire night in prayer {Lk. 6:12-13}. There are times when we must make momentous decisions which will affect the rest of our lives. In such hours, we need divine guidance. We should turn to God's word to see what it speaks on the subject, seek out the best counsel you can find. {Pro. 11:14}, "Where no counsel is, the people fall: but in the multitude of counselors there is safety"}. And to ask God's direction in our lives, James said, "If any one of you lack wisdom, let him ask of God, that gives to all men liberally, and upbraids not; and it shall be given him" {James 1:5}. The Lord will help us to make these decisions when we ask for his guidance.

WHEN WE ARE DISCOURAGED:—We should not quit. We need to turn to God in prayer. Jesus said, "Men ought to pray always, and not to faint" {Lk. 18:1}. Paul said, "Praying always with all prayers and supplication in the Spirit, and watching thereunto with all perseverance and supplication for all saints", {Eph. 6:18}. When we are discouraged, let us ask God to send us some help in the form of other Christians.

WHEN WE HAVE EVIL THOUGHT:—Sometimes circumstances fill our minds with evil thoughts, even without our premeditation. When we find that occurring, we can either allow those thoughts to stay in our minds which will likely lead us to sin or we can drive them out through prayer and meditation upon God's word. We cannot keep birds from flying over our heads, but we can prevent them from nesting in our hair. In the same way, we cannot prevent every temptation, but can keep ourselves from dwelling on these evil thoughts.

WHEN WE HAVE SINNED:—John instructed us to pray for forgiveness of our sins. He said, "But if we walk in the light, as he is in the light, we have fellowship one with another, and the blood of Jesus Christ his Son cleanse us from all sins. If we say we have not sin, we deceive ourselves, and the truth is not in us. If we confess our sins, he is faithful and just, to forgive us our sins, and to cleanse us from all unrighteousness" {1Jn. 1:7-9}. God has made forgiveness of sins conditional to his erring children. They must repent of them and pray that both their deeds and their intention to commit them might be forgiven, {Act. 8:22}.

Here are sometimes that we should especially be taking our requests to God in prayer. Remember the words of Paul when he wrote that we should "pray without ceasing" {1Thess. 5:17}.

HOW TO HAVE YOUR PRAYERS ANSWERED

a. THANKSGIVING AND PRAISES {WORSHIP}

The word of God teaches us that before we approach the Great God the Father, we should give thanks and praises to him. "Enter his gate with thanksgiving and his court with praise, give thanks to him and praise his name", {Psalm 100:4}. It is our command to communicate with our Father, initially, by giving him thanks, and sing praises to his holy name before we tell him all our needs. Jesus thought the disciples, and not to them only but to us also, how we should begin our prayer life. He did not begin with forgiveness or any other thing in the course of the prayer, but rather, he started with "This, then, is how you should pray: "Our Father in heaven, hallowed be your name", {Matthew 6:9}. The Lord Jesus Christ demonstrated to us to start hallowing the Father in our prayer life before we get to him.

b. FORGIVENESS

This has been a great blow to many Christians of not receiving from the Lord. Watch this and sow it into your spirit, that unforgiving is a spirit which flows from the pit of a hell which Satan uses to attack the body of Christ. It is the greatest element to hinder our blessings from the Lord. In the book Mark chapter 11, made it known to us that if we do not forgive our neighbors, our prayers will not ascend to the throne of God, "And when you stand praying, if you hold anything against anyone, forgive them, so that your Father in heaven may forgive you your sins" {Mark 11:25-26}. Do not pray to God if your neighbor has any issue against you, for it derails your answers from the Lord. All what you need is to make peace with him, and ask God for forgiveness and your prayers will be heard as Jesus said, "Therefore, if you are offering your gift at the altar and there remember that your brother has something against you, leave your gift there in front of the altar. First, go and be reconciled to your brother, then come and offer your gift" {Matthew 5:23-24}.

c. REPENTANCE

Bear in mind that you are confronting the holy God who does not look at sin in any aspect of life, so your mind-set should be renewed. It will be well with you "That you put off concerning the former conversation the old man, which is corrupt according to the deceitful lust; and be renewed in the spirit of your mind; and that you put on the new man, which after God is created in righteousness and true holiness {Ephesians 4:22-24}.

We are sinful therefore we need to repent from our sins before we can approach the holy God. As the high priests of old were cleansed with the blood of a lamb as a sacrifice, so as our sins are wiped away if we confess our sins and ask for forgiveness through the blood of our Lord Jesus Christ. The atoning blood of Jesus Christ cleanse us from all unrighteousness and we become as holy as never sinned when we confess our sins, for it is written, "I, even I, am he who blots out your transgressions, for my own sake, and remembers your sins no more", {Isaiah 43:25}. And David said "blessed is the one whose sin the Lord does not count against them and in whose spirit is no deceit" {Psalm 32:2}.

d. PRAY IN THE NAME OF JESUS

You might be asking, why should we only pray in the name of Jesus? Hear me beloved, all the authority of the God-head has been embodied in that name, "For in Christ all the fullness of the Deity lives in the bodily form" {Colossians 2:9}. Now the Lord Jesus himself is at the right hand of God in heaven. And how majesty and powerful he is in heaven, so is his name operating in the realm of the spirit. The name of Jesus became ever powerful, to resolve every problem on the earth when it was highly exalted above every name. "Therefore, God also has highly exalted him, and given him a name which is above every name, that at the name of Jesus every knee should bow, of things in heaven, and things in earth, and things under the earth", {Philippians 2:9-10}.Our Lord Jesus gave us the key to receive answer to our prayers from the heavenly Father only through his exalted name, as he said, "And in that day you shall ask me nothing Verily, verily, I say unto you, whatsoever you shall ask in my NAME, he will give it you" {John 16:23}. Pray not to any other name to your Father who is in heaven than the name of Jesus.

e. FIND THE WORD WHICH SUIT YOUR PROBLEM

You cannot just be on your knee and communicate to God without having your word of remembrance {the word of to use in prayer} ready. Prayer is the communication between you and God pleading together, and it can be done only when you remember him his word of promise, "Put me in remembrance; let us contend together; state your case, that you may be proved right" {Isaiah 43:26}. The lord is expecting you to come to him with his word which will serve as a stepping stone to intervene in your situation.

Jesus made an emphasis concerning this in the gospel of John. It was vividly elaborated that to achieve our wishes from the throne of God, we should abide in his word. It enlightens us to look nowhere than to depend on the word of God, "If you remain in me and my words

remain in you, ask whatever you wish, and it will be done for you"
{John 15:7}. Sow in your spirit that when the word of God goes out,
it does not return empty but rather it fulfils all the purposes it is sent
for, "So is my word that goes out of my mouth; it will not return to
me empty, but will accomplish what I desire and achieve the purposes
for which I sent it", {Isaiah 55:11}. There is a word of God reserved for
you in the Bible to be used, for you to put the Lord in remembrance
in order to intervene in your case. Though he knows everything about
you, but yet, he is expecting you to come before him with his word
of promises.

f. SET THE GOD KIND OF FAITH IN MOTION

This is the moment of time that God is watching you to release
to you, your heart desire which you are pouring before him. Hear
me holiness is what God is expecting his people to attain in his
kingdom, because without it you cannot get closer to him. Yes that
is true, but your holiness cannot touch the heart of God to release to
you your answer to the prayer. It takes faith, for without it, you will
just afflict your self for nothing, "And without faith, it is impossible
to please God, because anyone who comes to him must believe that
he exist and that he REWARDS those who earnestly seek him,
{Hebrew 11:6}.

There are many levels of faith, but the faith which moves much the
hand of God is what we called the great faith. It is that faith which
the Canaanite woman from Tyre and Sidon   demonstrated for the
healing of his daughter who was tormented by the devil. Jesus said to
her, "Oh woman, your "faith is great"; it shall be done for you as you
wish. And her daughter was healed at once" {Read from Matthew 15;
21-28}. This kind of faith can only be achieved when you release all what
you believe and trust in your innermost being to the Lord. The Lord
is waiting for you to come to him with this kind of faith for answering
your prayers.

g. PRAY IN THE SPIRIT

Jesus declared to us the kind of God whom we are worshipping, in the gospel of John. It was revealed that God is a spirit, and as we were created in his likeness, we need to go to him in like manner. Jesus said, the true worshippers which the heavenly Father is seeking to worship him are those who are spiritual, "God is a spirit; and they that worship him must worship him in spirit and in truth" {John 4:24}.

If we have a look at the book of Ephesians, it states that we should go the Father in the Spirit, "Praying all always with all prayer and supplication in the Spirit" {Ephesians 4:16}. Jude also made it clearly that "But you, beloved, building up yourselves on your most holy faith, praying in the Holy Ghost" {Jude 20}. The word of God says, "In the mouth of two or three witnesses shall a thing be established" {2nd Corinthians 13:1}.

The reason the Lord is telling us to pray in the Spirit is that it takes the Spirit to know how we can touch the real heart of God because the Lord knows the mind of the Spirit. The Spirit prays through us more than we do because he is our intercessor, "Likewise the Spirit also helps our infirmities; for we know not what we should pray for as we ought; but the Spirit itself makes intercession for us with groaning which cannot be uttered", {Romans 8:26}.

Many people usually say "they pray according to the will of God". Yes! I do believe, but the question is, do they know the mind of God more than the Spirit of God? NO! Then why not pray in the Spirit so that the Spirit will pray according to the will of God?

"And he that searches the hearts knows what is the mind of the Spirit, because he makes intercession for the saints ACCORDING TO THE WILL OF GOD" {Romans 8:27}.

THANK THE LORD TO HAVE ANSWERED YOUR PRAYERS

Jesus said, "It shall be done according to your faith" {Matthew 9:29}. Now you have believed that God has answered all what you prayed for, because Jesus said, "Therefore I tell you, whatever you ask for in prayer, believe that you have received it, and it will be yours", {Mark 11:24}. You have believed and received your answer to the prayer by faith therefore all what has left is giving thanks to the Lord, to have answered your prayer.

The problem of the Christians today is that once they have believed by faith that the Lord has answered their prayers, they continue praying the same prayer in every blessed day. That is not the prayer of faith but rather unbelief. You might say, what am I saying? Now, for example, if you need a pen urgently to write something down and I give it to you, will you ask me again to give you another pen at that moment? If no, then what are you going to tell me when I give it to you? Are you not going to thank me for giving the pen? So it is in prayer when you believe by faith that the Lord has answered your prayers, All you have to do is to thank him and glorify his name for what he has done for you. You will continue with thanksgiving till it is manifested physically rather than to continue repeating the same thing which you believed.

A GUIDE TO SUCCESSFUL FASTING AND PRAYERS PAGES

a. WEIGH YOUR PURPOSE

There is an adage which say, "A toad does not run in the daytime for nothing". It means that nothing in this universe happens by chance. If there is a reason for everything on this planet, then there is a need to value whatever you intend to do in your life cycle. To afflict your body has a great importance in life, and the question is that, is it an easy task?

If not then you have to make up your mind that by hook or crook, you have to achieve the purpose of your fasting, "For our light affliction, which is but for a moment, works for us a far more exceeding and eternal weight of glory" {2Corinthians 4:17}.

Don't let anything move you or distract you from achieving your goal in the affliction of your body, because the grace of God will be sufficient for you and the power of God will make you perfect in weakness. Once you have made a real decision to fast, believe with all your heart that "The afflicted shall eat and be satisfied, those who seek him shall praise the Lord! May your heart live forever" {Psalm 22:26}

b. KNOW THE KIND OF FASTING

There are many types of fasting in the kingdom of God. We have what we called dry fasting. In this type of fasting, no food or drink is needed. The issue is that, when you live up to three days without food and drink the intestines can cause damage to your health so you may need a little water to sustain you ahead to continue your dry fasting. This kind of fasting are those who are seeking for the anointing or the power of God.

In addition, we have what we call water fasting. In this kind of fasting, you can drink water in the course of the fasting but not as much as to fill up your stomach to the brim. And then also, we have fruit fasting, porridge and others. It depends on how you like it.

Daniel demonstrated vegetables and water fasting when he was in the kings Palace in Babylon when he said to the eunuchs, "Prove your servants, I beseech you, ten days; and let them give us pulse to eat and water to drink" {Daniel 1:12}. And in the ten chapter, he ate but not pleasant food, "In those days I Daniel was mourning three full weeks, I ate no pleasant bread, neither came flesh nor wine in my mouth, neither did I anoint myself at all" {Daniel 10:3}.

It is your own decision to choose which one you think you can make it. It is done according to ones ability or strength.

c. WEIGH YOUR HEALTH CONDITION

Fasting is something which does not go under compulsion. Not every one has the same strength to do the same fasting. Don't ever say all the people are doing so you are going to compare yourself to do the same. That is wrong motive which can affect tremendously your healthy condition. You can choose to eat but not your pleasant food as Daniel did. You can eat any food but not you usually eat as your pleasant food and it will be accepted by the Lord because he knows all what you are going through concerning your life

d. SET A GOAL OF HOW LONG IT WILL FAST

To set a goal about your fasting, it depends on your ability to withstand long days. Sit and weigh your strength if you can cope with long days or not. There have been many people who have died in the course of the fasting. People usually imitate people forgotten that all hands are not equal. Some men of God who tried to imitate the Lord Jesus for forty days miss the mark, of not eating and drinking, which caused their death at the end.

We don't follow what people do but what you can do or achieve because fasting is not a competition as a whole.

Don't ever let anybody dictate for you how you should fast. Make the decision by yourself because it is not that fellow who is going to fast for you. Church can declare fast for the whole congregation but it is you who will decide the one you will choose, either dry fasting, fruit or water for the sake of you health.

e. AVOID PHARASEISM

Fasting and prayer is something that we do to the secret God whom we don't see. God who is a Spirit rewards in things done in secret places like giving, fasting and praying.

Jesus condemned the Pharisees way of fasting because they did it to gain glory from men instead of God. Jesus said, "Moreover, when you fast, do not be like the hypocrites with a sad countenance. For they disfigure their faces that they may appear to men to be fasting. Assuredly, I say to you, they have their reward" {Matthew 6:16}. Fasting is not an outward show but secret thing which the Lord is expecting from his people. Don't let people know that you are fasting, but if you have somebody like your spiritual father or any man of God whom you trust, you can inform him to be your help as an intercessor to your need. In your working place, don't let the people know that you are fasting, even when they ask you, tell them that you are okay. Make your countenance look as good as usual, "But you when you fast, anoint your head and wash your face so that your fasting will not be noticed by men, but by your Father who is in secret; and your Father who sees what is done in secret will reward you" {Matthew 6:17-18}.

f. SELF-CONTROL

The devil does not want you to succeed in your affliction, for he knows that when you come out of it, the Lord is going to bless you. You will be tempted all the way around but sin not for it is written "Blessed is the man who remain steadfast under the trial, for when he has stood the test he will receive the crown of life, which God has promised to those who love him" {James 1:12}, The moment he sees that you are much focus on the Lord he will do well to send somebody to bother you in order to distract you from the focus that you have been engaged towards the Lord, usually when you are at your working place. When you confront such a problem in your working place, be patient and endure to the end and you will wear a crown of life, "Therefore, seeing we also are compassed about with so great a cloud of witnesses, let us lay aside every weight, and the sin which do so easily beset us, and let us run with patience the race that is set before us" {Hebrew 12:1}. When you confront any problems, don't retaliate but rather think about what you are going to achieve from the Lord at the end of your prayers, and stay calm and the good Lord will see you through. "Only let your conversation be as it becomes the gospel of Christ" {Philippians 1:27}.

g. STUDY THE WORD OF GOD

This is one of the major parts of fasting and prayer. Fasting without the word is not complete because it is the word of God which consist all things in the fasting. If visions or revelations will come, it is revealed through and according to the word of God. As you begin to study the word of God, the Spirit of the Living God also will start revealing things to you in the dreams visions and the revelations, and also the revelation knowledge will follow the suit. Revelation knowledge does not manifest unless the Holy Spirit takes the word in you and reveal it to you concerning the thing which needed to be revealed to you.

The word of God should be the backbone of your fasting so the Bible should be around you study.

h. PRAY FERVENTLY

If possible, you can pray in every two or three hours in between. The reason is that the more you pray, the more you move in the spiritual realm. That is to say, the more you aglow in the spirit. Fasting without prayers is like fetching water with a basket with holes, be on your guard to pray fervently to achieve your goal. Bear in mind that you are afflicting your body to achieve something valuable from God.

IMPORTANCE OF FASTING

1. IT RENEWS THE SPIRIT

When fasted, the beginning of the whole process portraits the growth of the inner man, It strikes a blow to the flesh and put it under subjection, {1Corinthians 9:27}. In the actual sense, the spirit and the flesh play mastery of themselves. Each one fights to rule the other when it is allowed, "For the flesh lusts against the Spirit, and the Spirit against the flesh and these are contrary the one to the other so that you cannot do the things that you would" {Galatians 5:17}. Know for sure that it is in the flesh where Satan dominates and the result of it is carnality which is against the things of the Spirit.

Fasting and prayer therefore is the only way to overcome the flesh, and when the Spirit rules the flesh, you are no more under condemnation, {Romans 8:1}.

2. GROWTH IN FAITH

Let us analyze the scripture of Romans 10:17. It says, "So then faith comes by hearing, and hearing by the word of God". Most Christians think the word of God {Logos} is what the Bible is talking about. They take it to be a written word, which is the Logos. The Logos can impart faith to you unless Rhema comes out of what you are reading. The growth of the faith is by hearing the spoken word of the Lord through his word. Fasting helps hearing the voice of the Lord even when studying the word of God, and it will boost you up in the growth of faith.

3. IT NECESSITATE TO THE SENSITIVE TO THE SPIRIT

There are nine gifts which the Lord has given to the church for edification, {1Corinthians 12:7-10}. Fasting and prayer is the only way to boost up the manifestations of the nine gifts of the Spirit. The moment you fast and pray you will begin to sense the manifestation of the Spirit in you and in your body, and the operation of the Spirits begins function.

4. IT HELPS GET CLOSER TO GOD IN HUMILITY

It is the major factor to get near to God by humility. Jesus was exalted and given a name that is above all names, for he humbled himself to the point of death, even to the cross, read Philippians 2:8-9. Humility is the key for the Lord to shower his blessings on his people. Only the humble ones are honored and exalted in the kingdom of Christ, for "The fear of the Lord is the instruction for wisdom, and before honor comes humility" {Proverb 15:33}.

Self denial is occurred when fasting and prayers are being practiced in ones life regularly. And it is the ultimate goal of every child of God to pursue in life as the Lord Jesus commanded us to do before we can be his disciple, {Matthew 16:24}. Fasting and prayers has therefore serves as the major factor to draw humanity to God.

5. IT BRINGS VISIONS AND REVELATIONS

Fasting and prayers are the catalyst of visions and revelations. You cannot experience visions and revelations from the Lord without involving in fasting. How was Daniel able to interpret dreams? He fasted and prayed fervently to the Lord of Host and the Lord revealed to him the interpretation of the dreams and the visions, Read Daniel chapter 2.

CHAPTER 6

UNDERSTANDING CHURCH LEADERSHIP

Leadership is very important to every organization as well as the church of God. Unfortunately, many Christians have the perception that knowing alone makes one a great leader. But what I want us to understand is that the bible is not a manual for leadership. In fact, when the concept of leadership does occur, it appears more often in terms of servant hood than in leadership. Moses, the great hero and leader of the Jewish people, was called "the servant of the Lord"

Very few Old Testament didactic portions deal directly with leadership. One could draw inference from certain recitations of the Law and Prophets and multitudinal guidelines from Proverbs and poetical literature. But none of these really represent didactic description of godly leadership. In the New Testament, several words connote the meaning of "govern" and "lead". A predominant word for leadership is the word hegeomai which means "to lead"; "to think"; "to believe"; "to regard as". In Hebrews, 13:24, the word hegoumenous was translated as "the leaders". The author greets the "leaders" before he greets "all God's people" which I Joshua 1:1. {new international version}.

Jesus as a model leader has taught a great deal of leadership in terms of servant hood. However, when it comes to defining "leadership" biblically, one has to delineate it from studying the lives of the people of

God. For this reason, the following questions are raised: "Is the subject of leadership biblical? Are there valid principals for organization and spiritual leadership? To these questions, the answer is yes. The bible, both the Old and the New Testaments, provide ample resources for establishing biblical leadership principles,

HOW TO UNDERSTAND BIBLICAL LEADERSHIP

1. Biblical leadership is a quality principal which God is seeking to use to accomplish his purpose at critical times in history. The Old Testament history shows that men like Moses, Joshua, David, Elijah, and Nehemiah were spiritual leaders God used in their respective generations to accomplish his divine purpose.

2. Biblical leadership does not denote infallibility of the leaders. On the contrary, almost all of the leaders whose lives were recorded in the bible have failures in one way or the other. But they were not defeated by their failures. They learned from their mistakes and rose up again victoriously.

3. Biblical leadership is invested in spiritual power and authority. And what is authority? Authority is the right to exercise leadership in a particular group or institution based upon a combination of qualities, characteristics, or expertise that a leader has or that followers believe their leader has. To exercise authority involves influencing, directing, coordinating, or otherwise guiding the thought and behavior of persons and groups in ways that they consider legitimate. Contrary to modern day thinking of equality in every realm, the biblical leaders were given by God the authority to exercise in regard to spiritual matters. For example, Elijah exercised his spiritual authority over King Ahab, and Nathan used his prophetic authority to convict David to the adultery he committed. Authority in leadership is a spiritual principle. The Christian leader should not be afraid to use it. Of course, there are also dangers of abusing authorities. Pastoral leaders are among those who easily get

on power trips. As Anthony Campolo, Jr. shares, "It may be that some were attracted to the ministry because they saw in the role of minister the opportunity to exercise power". Charles Jefferson says, "The Pastor is possessor of a power that is extraordinary and hence he must be evermore on his guard against the temptation to play the lord". It is always a dilemma the pastoral leadership has to face. One can either over use or under use power and authority. The wisdom that the pastoral leaders need to acquire and exercise is the careful guarding of the power and authority given to them.

4. Biblical leadership demands higher moral and spiritual standards. Jesus demonstrated a blameless life that no critic of His could find any fault in his life. Paul shared with the church in Thessalonica, "You are witnesses, and so is God, of how holy, righteous and blameless we were among you who believed." A leader's life and how he lives is more important than any other abilities or skills he may have. A secular leader may live in an immoral life and still function as an influential leader, but not as a pastoral leader. One cannot expect a pastoral leader to be perfect, but he must not defile himself morally or ethnically either. It is important that words and deeds of the pastoral leader give evidence of a life being transformed by Jesus Christ.

5. Biblical leadership is characterized by willing sacrifice. Jesus said, "For even the Son of Man did not come to be served, but to serve, and to give his life as a ransom for many". The trademark of spiritual leaders is that they are willing to sacrifice for the people they lead and serve. Moses sacrificed the privilege of going into Canaan because of Israel's disobedience and unbelief. Joshua decided to live among the people for the sake of winning the war. Paul suffered much for the sake of preaching the gospel to the lost world and for the benefit of the people he had led to the Lord.

6. Biblical leadership is described as servant hood. The words "leader" and "leadership" do not appear in the gospels. Jesus saw himself

as a servant. Jesus said to his disciples, "For who is greater, the one who is at the table or the one who serves? Is it not the one who is at the table? But I am among you as one who serves." Jesus refused the request of James and John's mother to seat her sons on His right and left, the leadership positions. The lack of the usage of "leader" and "leadership" in the gospels could well be that Jesus meant for the disciples to learn leadership by following rather than by commanding. Supervising, or managing.

7. Biblical leadership is mandated by the spirit of team work. Paul emphasized a distributive leadership among the people of God based on gifts or God-given abilities rather than on an authoritarian hierarchical structure. Paul saw Christian leadership as a part in the whole and a whole in parts. There is mutually among God's people; they all play an important role in the function of the body of Christ in their unique ways.

To be successful, effective, and fruitful in any institution, be it at home, business or church, one must operate based on principles. Principles that are not invented by us, or by society, but by the laws of the universe, that are pertain to human relationships, and human organizations.

They are part of human condition, consciousness, and conscienceness, principles that will apply at all times and in all places.

T. M Moore, the president of Chesapeake Theological Seminary made a list of seven principles of Biblical leadership, they are:

1. A leader is the one who understand his God-appointed calling more in terms of the results that are to be achieved than of the activities that will be required to achieve them

2. A leader is the one who is able to motivate, enlist, develop, and deploy others in the service of his God-appointed calling in a way that leads them to realize their own greatest potential for serving the Lord.

3. A leader is the one who is able to organize his work and his resources according to a strategically-focused plan.

4. A leader is the one who is able to persevere at his God-appointed calling, even in the face of setbacks, opposition, and seemingly insurmountable obstacles.

5. A leader is the one who has learned to be content with the thought that he may live to see the completion of his God-appointed calling.

6. While leaders have sometimes been called to their tasks directly from the Lord himself, most often they arrive at this position only after an extended period of preparation, trials, and maturing.

7. A leader is the one who has a clear sense of the eternal context that the larger {than himself or his time} significance of the work he has been given to do. As Moses could free the Israelites in the land of milk and honey, so a leader should have a vision and envision the results that lay ahead. Leadership is not just finishing his own goals, it is also developing other so they can lead, as it is said, "the greatest reward a leader can achieve—the greatest legacy a leader can leave—is a group of talented, self-confident, and cooperative people, who are themselves ready to lead". Walter Lippmann, one of the greatest writers of all time wrote upon the death of Franklin Delano Roosevelt that, "The final test of a leader is that he leaves behind him the other men the conviction and the will to carry on.

PRINCIPLES FOR LEADERSHIP

The Biblical principles of leadership, is certainly best modeled by our Lord and Jesus Christ.

When Jesus talks about leadership, he begins with servant hood, which he demonstrated by his own humility. A few hours before his crucifixion, his disciples got into a quarrel; they fought for prominence, as Luke recorded, "A dispute arose among them {his disciples} as to which of them was considered to be greatest. Jesus said to them, "The kings of the Gentiles lord it over them; and those who exercise authority over them call themselves Benefactors, but you are not to be like that. Instead, the greatest among you should be like the youngest, and the one who rules like the one who serves. For who is greater, the one who is at the table or the one who serves? Is not the one who is at the table? But I am among you as the one who serves.

It is inconceivable that the very disciples of Jesus could do something like that at that crucial moment, yet it is indisputable true. Human nature will always strive for prestige, importance and position. It is during those occasions that Jesus used the opportunity to teach his disciples what true leadership and greatness mean. In Jesus' mind, true greatness is not the one who is being served, but the one who serves. That is why he said in the gospel of Mark, "For even the Son of Man did not come to be served, but to serve, and give his life as ransom for many" {Mark 10:25}.

Jesus not only thought his disciples to be servants, He himself demonstrated it at the last super for washing each and everyone of his disciples' feet. Jesus humbled himself before he was highly exalted by the God the Father. Peter exhorted the young men of his day, "Humble your selves therefore, under God's mighty hand, that he may lift you up in due time." {1Peter 5:6}. Leadership starts from knee high. When the disciples disputed among themselves, it indicated that they only had themselves in mind that they did not think of others, that they had no concern for others, as one of them might be their leader. Instead, they fought for themselves as to who should take the prominent position, since "we all are on equal footing".

Jesus did not appoint anyone of them to be the team leader, but he did ask the thought—providing question, "Who among you is the greatest". If anyone is humble enough, he will not answer, "I am'! As a matter of fact, in Jesus' crowd, there is no one who is the greatest. The greatest is Jesus; but he acted and lived as a servant of all. A B Oswald Sanders observes, "True greatness, true leadership, is achieved not by reducing men to one's service but in giving oneself in selfless service to them".

THE PRINCIPLE OF SACRIFICE

Jesus offered himself as a ransom for many. Leadership always comes with a price, a price to pay for the responsibility that comes with it. The concept of incarnation is not new in Christian thought, but it is unique in leadership thinking. When God became man-Jesus, who descended from heaven, he took a giant step to identify Himself with the people. He was to lead. Leighton Ford says, "Here is a leader who is one with us; in Jesus, God has totally identified himself with us. Jesus sacrificed his prestige, high position of being equal with God, glory, and many privileges to come down to the earth. He took upon himself the human form and became a servant". Leighton Ford added in this way: the most spectacular leadership in the history of humanity took place when the Son of Man became first-century Galilean Jew. In that identification, he renounced the status and the rights that he enjoyed as God's Son. Among them, Jesus gave up any right to independence. He was born in a borrowed manger, preached from borrowed boat, entered Jerusalem on a borrowed donkey, ate the Last Supper at a borrowed upper room, died on a borrowed cross and was buried in a borrowed tomb." In renouncing entitlement, He exposed himself to temptation, sorrow, limitation and pain.

By such sacrifices, Jesus became a bottom-up leader and shouldered all the pains and difficulties of others, in order that others may be more effective, and that they may reach their potentials.

PRINCIPLE OF SUFFERING

When James and John requested the higher position to sit next to Jesus on the left and right, Jesus challenged them as to whether or not they would drink the bitter cup. They both promised that they could. But sanders is right when he comments that, their glib answer "We are able"—betrayed a tragic lack of self-knowledge. When the time came for the test, they ran away from it. Jesus had to take up the bitter cup, to suffer for the sake of his followers and all mankind. It is through suffering that he reached the top. God has exalted him to the highest place and gave him the name that is above every name.

"Ministry that costs nothing, accomplish nothing", says John Henry Jowett. Suffering is part of the ministry, so it is part of leadership."

Jesus said, "The man who loves his life will loose it, while the man who hates his life in this world will keep it for eternal life. Whosoever serves me must follow me; and where I am, my servant also will be. My Father will honor the one who serve me", {Jn 12:25-26}.

THE PRINCIPLE OF SUBMISSION

At the garden of Gethsemane, as He faced death on the cross, Jesus had to struggle like a humane being. But in the end, He submitted himself to God, and allowed God's will to be done. He said, "Abba Father, everything is possible for you. Take this cup from me, yet not what I will, but what you will." {Luke 22:42}. Jesus as a Son of God could use his power to do whatever he wanted to do, but he never acted as if he had it all. He gave his right to be right, and died on the cross. Spiritual leadership demands that one not think his way is the only way. Submission is not an indication of weakness; on the contrary, it is the sign of strength. Only the ones who know how to submit to authority know how to be in authority.

"No person who is not under authority has the right to exercise authority", says Warren Wiersbe. He also made a good comparison between submission and subjugation. He states, "Subjugation turns a person into a thing, destroys individuality, and removes all liberty." Submission makes a person become more of what God wants him to be; it brings out individuality; it gives him the freedom to accomplish all that God has for life and ministry.

Submission is strength; it is the first step toward true maturity and ministry.

To be a leader, one must understand the meaning of submission. There is power in the secret of submission. Jesus in submitting himself to the authority of God, won the world for God.

THE PRINCIPLE OF SOVEREINGTY

Oswald Sanders initiated his taught; "Sovereignty in terms of God taking the initiative to appoint leaders. It is not of anyone's choice, but by God's appointment." "Sanders argue; "No theological training or leadership course will automatically confer spiritual leadership or qualify one for an effective ministry." Jesus was later to tell them, "You did not choose me, but I choose you, and appoint you" {Jn 15:16}. To be able to affirm, "I am not here by selection of a man or the election of a group, but by the sovereign appointment of God", gives great confidence to the Christian workers.

Jesus came by not his own will, but by the will of the Father and to do his will. Scripture abounds, in this regard Jesus said many times that he was sent by the Father to accomplish God's purpose. Jesus said, "My food is to do the will of whom who sent me and to finish his work" {Jn 4:34}. It is clear that spiritual leadership is entrusted not by self-initiation, but by divine appointment.

THE PRINCIPLE OF SHARING

This is in fact one of the areas killing the vision of many leaders in God's work in this dispensation. But we shouldn't forget that Jesus never thought of doing his work all by himself. From the very beginning of his earthly ministry, He had chosen men to be with him. He trained them to work with him, and later to continue his ministry. As it is well known, he had three of the twelve disciples that were considered to be his "inner circle"

They always went as a team. They shared the responsibility. They built up each other, with Jesus as their leader and teacher.

Bible leadership requires that work be done not by one man but a group of men. When Moses was in charge of ruling the Israelites day and night, his father-in-law, Jethro visited him. Jethro observed all what Moses was doing, and immediately noticed Moses' problem. Moses did not have a support group, he did not know how to delegate his responsibilities, he did not build a team work with him, and even, he did not share his ministry with other capable men. So Jethro suggested, what he was doing was not good. You and these people who come to you would be wearing out. The work was heavy for Moses and cannot handle alone. He told him, "listen to me and I would give you some advise, and may God be with you, in your leadership role".

You must be people's representative before God and bring their disputes to him. Teach them the decrees and the laws, and show them the way to live, and the duties they to perform. But select capable men from all the tribes-men who fear God, trustworthy men who hate dishonest gain-and appoint them as officials over thousands, hundreds, fifties, and tens. Have them bring every difficult case to you; the simple themselves. That will make your load lighter, because they will share it with you. If you do this and God so commands, you will be able to stand the strain, and all these people will go home satisfied. Jethro, a gentile priest, knew more about leadership than his son-in-law, Moses a man of God. Jethro's advise lightened Moses ministry burden, and it also set an important principle for the future leaders. To be effective in leadership responsibility, one must learn how to share with others, and let other capable people take part in building up the church of God.

THE PRINCIPLE OF SUCCESSION

As someone has said, "success without a successor is failure." A good leader always develops, and prepares others to take his place. It can be said that one works oneself out of a job. Jesus spent three years training and discipline of twelve men for the task he would leave behind for them to accomplish. The Bible is filled with good examples of successful leadership transition. A few examples will suffice the purpose here. Moses and Joshua, Joshua had followed Moses for at least forty years as his assistant. Now, Moses was about to pass away from the scene, and Joshua was well prepared by Moses. When the time came for transition, it went so well that could command as good of a lead as Moses.

Scripture recorded that; "Now Joshua son of Nun, was filled with Spirit of wisdom because Moses has laid his hands on him. So the Israelites listened to him and did what the Lord had commanded Moses." {Deut. 34:9}. It is not easy, to see one's successor more successful than himself. But Moses did it nicely with gracious humility. He was the one that set the goal to enter into Canaan, but it was Joshua who actually led the Israelites in, and Moses died before his dream was realized.

A great leader care more about what God wants to accomplish than through whom he will accomplish it.

ELIJAH AND ELISHA; one of the dramatic Biblical records of a leader and follower relationship is illustrated by these two men. Elisha's desired to follow Elijah, even to the last minute, has earned him the privilege to succeed the great prophet and carry on the important ministry that Elijah left him. Without knowing, Elisha has fulfilled God's appointment of him, when God said to Elijah, to anoint Elisha, son of Shaphat from Abel Meholah to succeed you as a prophet.

PAUL AND TIMOTHY; Paul was a leader that made leaders. Both his life and in his teachings depict his desires to develop future leaders. Paul not only discharged his leadership responsibility to Timothy, he also charged him to develop others as leaders: And the things you have heard me say in the presence of many witness, entrusted to reliable men who will also be qualified to teach others. To survive and grow, a movement such as the Christian faith must be at least four-deep: Paul mentored Timothy, who was in turn asked to mentor others, {2 Timothy 2:2}, who would still mentor others—four layers of successors, who really did spread the infant movement, eventually to every continent.

Jesus three years of active ministry on earth was to find, select, and disciple the twelve men to succeed him for a task that will eventually turn the world upside down.

CHAPTER 7

THE LIGHT BRINGS GOALS

INTRODUCTION

For the purpose of this book, this is indeed one of the important and crucial areas needs to be looked at carefully because it has a lot to do with our natural and church leadership. The reason is that a leader without set goals is like a pilot without a compass. There are two kinds of goal one can set in life: There are BE goals; and there are DO goals. Goals come in all kinds, types, and sizes. It's useful to see that some goals have to do with what we want to be, and others have to do with what we want to do. The be goals have to do with our attributes, such as lovingness, kindness, righteousness, honesty, etc. they also have to do with our position, such as mother, businessman, worker. The do goals are the things we want to accomplish or the actions we want to take. Goals are not isolated incidents in life. it is important to see them as a whole, all goals are interconnected with each other. One cannot separate his business goals from his family goals or from his Christian service. All must be taken together.

1. WHAT IS A GOAL?

This is one of the questions almost everyone on earth asks at some point in their lives. And the answers we get to this question vary from one another base on how we see the picture. But for the purpose of this teachings, let me help you with some few definitions. A goal is something toward which to aim. A goal is a target. A goal is a specific purpose worth working towards. A goal is a desired outcome that can be measured in terms of progress toward an objective. A goal is a statement of faith, how one hopes things are going to be at some time in the future.

2. WHY SET GOALS?

Having known the various definitions of goals, there is the need to study why goal setting is important to every Christian leader. To some Christian leaders, their thinking is that the Christian life is controlled by God and His Holy Spirit. They just have to listen to His still small voice and obey. Wherever He leads, they will follow. Goals are not necessary, so they question the values of goals, and they are concerned about man's intrusion in God's plan. It is obvious that the scripture is not against goal setting. Paul said, "Therefore, I do not run like a man running aimlessly; I do not fight like a man beating the air" {1Corinthians 9:26}. Jesus also praised the shrew manager who set goals and made plans for his future, in the event, he should be fired by his boss, {Luke 16:1-8}. There is power in goal setting. Now, let's look at some of the reasons why there must be set goals in every leadership.

GOALS CAN MOTIVATE:—A person with clear and strong goals can overcome "confusion and conflict over incompatible values, contradictory desires and frustrated relationship with friends and relatives, all of which often result from the absence of rational strategies." With high and noble goals, one is motivated to strive forward and accomplish great things in life.

GOALS GIVE A SENSE OF DIRECTION:—Goals give one something to aim for. Goals help one to know where he is heading. Goals provide direction for one to work towards.

GOALS CHLLENGE ONE TO PLAN AHEAD:—Goals will help one to look to the future instead of focusing attention on the past. With the future in view one will not procrastinate and one will be challenge to accomplish every day's work, so one can reach one's goals.

GOALS HELP ONE TO FOCUS:—As there are many attractions and distractions in life, without goals, life could head towards many directions, and end up somewhere one did not expect to end up. Clearly defined goals will help one to concentrate and focus on things that need to be accomplished.

GOALS ARE GUIDE POSTS TO INDICATE PROGRESS:—Life is a long journey without road signs, so one can hardly know how far he has gone. Goals are segments of life's long objective. They give indications of progress. Goals give one a sense of knowing where one is in comparison to total journey.

GOALS PROVIDE STANDARDS OF EVALUATION:—Without goals, one will not know where one has been and how one has been doing in accomplishing what is expected. Goals will make one see that one is moving toward them.

GOALS GIVE THE POWER TO LIVE ON NOW:—The future is really not under anyone's control. No one knows what is going to happen in the future. However, goals are directions with the future in mind, but the future begins with today. A wise and powerful living of the now will bring one into the future. I hope this will help you to know why you need a goal as a leader.

3. HOW TO SET GOALS

SPECIFIC:—An objective may be massive and general. But a goal must be in exact terms. In order words, a goal is a statement that is clearly defined, "I want to buy a red delicious apple." Its specification is that it is a "red", not a "golden", delicious apple which one wants to buy.

ATTAINABLE:—A goal must be something that can be reached. If a church has a two hundred capacity congregation, and the average attendance of the Sunday worship service is one hundred and fifty, and the Pastor encourage each one to bring five people to church next Sunday, that is unattainable goal for two reasons; not everyone will have five unbelievable friends, and even if each one can bring five people to church, the sanctuary will not be able to accommodate them. A goal must a valid goal.

MEASURABLE:—"I want to buy two pounds of red delicious apples today" is a measurable goal. One can know whether it is one pound or two pounds by weighing it on a scale. By the end of the day, one can measure whether he has bought the apples or not.

Besides these basic criteria, goals should be dated, so that one will know whether he has accomplished the goal by that date. Deadlines often serve as motivators and force one to push forward. To be clear and exact, goals should be written down. Written goals serve as reminders and check lists to see far one has progressed or how many of the goals have been accomplished.

CHAPTER 8

THE NATURE OF GOD

INTRODUCTION

The ultimate life of humanity depends on God who created us for his glory, {Isaiah 43:7}. To enjoy the life of without sorrow, {proverb 10:22}, and arise and shine in your life potentials depend ultimately on God who created you and formed you from your mothers womb.

Which God are we talking about? Are we talking about the god of Buddha, the god of Mohammed, the god Hindu, or any other god who cannot even move his leg? I am talking about the God of Abraham, the God of Isaac, and the God of Jacob who created the heaven and the earth who faints not, and there is no searching of his understanding, {Isaiah 40:28}.

This is one of the sensitive topics that generate more debates among secular and religious thinkers. It has often been said that every human being has a "God shaped vacuum" inside them—everyone has a God-consciousness, although many apparently suppress it {Rom. 1: 20-21}. Yet even Christians, who do acknowledged the reality of God, often hold to a great variety of ideas about what He is like. In fact, many of these ideas conflict with each other and also with what the Bible actually teaches. But if our belief in God is to be rational, then it follows that our conception of who, and what, God Is should be coherent. If we claim to know God and love Him, then, it stands to reason that our understanding of God should match what He has revealed about Himself both generally in the natural world and specifically in the scriptures.

At this point, we are going to discuss some of the basic information about God to understand who God is and what He is like-His nature and His character.

THE NATURE OF GOD

The Bible portrays that we are the image of the invisible God. So the question remains, are we created the same as God? No! The reason is that the image the bible is saying in the book of Genesis 1: 27, "So God created man in his own image, in the image of God created he him; male and female created he them". When the bible says, we are the image of God it does not necessarily mean that God has the same attributes as we are. We are spiritual being, having a soul, and living in the body. Our spiritual beings were derived from Adam when God breathed his life into him, the breath of life and he became a living soul,{ Genesis 2: 7}.

THE GREAT MYSTERY

GOD IS A SPIRIT

So the question is, are we as the same as God, being a spiritual beings? No!

God is a Spirit, {Jn 4:24}. It means that he has none of the physical constraints associated with matter—He cannot be detected by our senses and he is immortal {1Timothy 1:17; 6:15-16}, and he is not limited to any particular geographical place or spatial location {Acts 17:24}. Yet many scriptures seem to indicate that God has a physical body. For example, He is described as having hands {Exodus 15:17}, feet {Psalm 110:1}, ears {Exodus 3:7; Isaiah 59:1b}.

GOD IS SELF-EXISTENT AND ETERNAL

There is no deity on this planet compared to Him because he is the ultimate controller of everything on this planet. God has no needs-nothing is necessary for him. His self existence is described in the Psalm 102: 24, and Psalm 102:12 adds; "But you, O LORD, sit enthroned forever; your renown endures through all generations." God's eternal nature is indicated in {Jn 1:1; 5:26, 8:58; and Colossians 1:16}.

GOD IS A PERSON

God is a person in nature. He is self-conscious and has a will, feelings can choose, and can relate to other personal beings. He acts in a personal way; He acts in a personal way; He speaks {Gen. 1:3}, sees {Gen. 11:5}, hears {Psalm 94:9}, grieves, {Gen. 6:6}, get angry {Deut. 1:37}, get jealous, {Exodus 20:5}, and is compassionate, {Psalm 111:4}.

THE TRIUNE GOD

The doctrine of the trinity {i.e. One God, but three persons} is a central element of Historic Christians. Although, the words "trinity" and "triune" are never mentioned anywhere in the Bible, and the doctrine is never explicitly taught anywhere in the scripture but there are many verses which strongly indicate that God is, indeed, triune. Not only the Father presented as God, {Matt. 6:26-32; Isaiah 9:6; Malachi 2:10; John 6:27; 45-46; 13:3; 16:27-28; 20:17; Romans 15:6; 1Corinthians 8:6; 15:24; Galatians 1:1; Ephesians 4:6; Philippians 2:11; Colossians 3:17; 1 Thessalonians 1:1}.

Jesus also is equated with God {2Peter 1:1; Titus 2:13; John 1; John 8:58; Matt. 26:63-65}. In addition, in John 20:28, Jesus did not rebuke Thomas for calling Him God, nor did he rebuke His disciples for worshipping Him {cf. Luke 4:8}, unlike the angel in Revelation 19:10; 22:8-10}.

Furthermore, the Spirit is also equated with God {1Corinthians 3:16; 12:4-11}. Indeed, Acts 5:3-4 equates lying to the Spirit is to lie to God. The Spirit also convicts {John 16:8-11} and regenerates {John 3:8} just as God does. Have in mind that, the personality of God implies a plurality of persons: personality does not develop nor exist in isolation, but only in association with other persons. Hence, it is not possible to conceive of personality in God apart from an association of equal persons in Him. Further evidence of the Trinity can be seen in the use of the plural form of "God" {Heb. Elohim} in passage such as Genesis 1:26; 11:7; and Isaiah 6:8. It is now clear that the plural noun represents multiple individual elements making up a single mass. In order words, three persons make up the God-head, in the same way that multiple individual humans make up humanity. Note, however, that while the persons of Trinity can be distinguished numerically as persons, they are indistinguishable and inseparable in their essence, substance and being. God is not composite, nor is He divisible in any issue.

God is immanent and transcendent:—Imminence is defined as {God's presence and activity within nature, human nature, and history. Transcendence, on the other hand, implies that "God is separate from and independent of nature and humanity.

God is immutable in person. He does not change. We should understand that the concept of a growing or evolving God is not found in the scriptures. Note, however, that immutability does not necessarily imply that God is sterile or static, but rather he is stable. His perfection and the fact that he stands outside of time, make it logically impossible for him to change. A perfect God can never improve or decline, and without time there can be no change in his state. Thus, not only does God's knowledge and plans {Psalm 33:11}, moral principles and will {Psalm 102:26-28} not change, neither does he have mood swings, nor do his affections and enthusiasm fade in intensity {James 1:17}, nor does his abhorrence of sin change {Malachi 3:1-6}. Although there may be changes around him and changes in his relationships, God does not change in his being

DIVINE ATTRIBUTES OF GOD

OMNIPRESECNCE:—the term "omnipresence" is borrowed from Latin. It is a compound of omni, meaning "all" and praesens, meaning "here. Thus, God is always here, close to everything, next to everyone. This means that God is unlimited with respect to space, as Wayne Grudem states that, "God doesn't have size or spatial dimensions and is present every point of space with his whole being, yet God acts differently in different places."

Indeed, the scriptures teaches that even though the highest heavens cannot contain God {1Kings 8:27}. He is still nearby when we pray, unlike the other gods, which don't even exist {Deut. 4:7}. Yet, God is not just nearby, He is in fact everywhere! He fills the heavens and the earth and no-one can hide from him. There are no secrets places where he is excluded {Jeremiah 23:23-24}. The psalmist summarizes this truth beautifully: "Where can I go from your Spirit? Where can I flee from your presence? If I go up to heavens, you are there; if I make my bed in the depths, you are there. If I rise on the wings, of the dawn, if I settle on the far side of the sea, even there your hand will guide me, your right hand will hold me fast" {Psalm 139:7-10, NIV}.

OMNISCIENT:—Again, the term "omniscience" is borrowed from Latin. It is also a compound of omni, meaning "all" and scienta, meaning "knowledge." Grudem explain it in this way: "God fully knows himself and all things actual and possible in one simple and external act." In order words, God is infinite in regard to knowledge. He knows himself and all other things perfectly {Job 37:16}, whether they be actual, or merely possible, throughout all of time {Isaiah 46:10; 1John 3:20b. He knows things immediately, simultaneously, exhaustively and truly. God knows all things perfectly, and he knows everything better than you and I because he created us.

OMNIPOTENT:—As with other omni terms, "omnipotence" is a Latin compound of omni, meaning "all" and potens, meaning "power," Grudem defines it in this way: "God's omnipotence means that God is able to do all his holy will." Omnipotence implies the possession of all power, and unlimited power. An omniscience God can do anything he pleases {Job 42:2} and is never exhausted. His power is unlimited in regard to both its extent and its magnitude. What is impossible for man is possible for God {Matthew 19:26}. Nothing is too hard for him {Jer. 32:17}. Further more, anything can be done as easily as anything else, and all acts are done effortlessly.

MERCYFUL AND GRACIOUS OF GOD

Mercy and grace are closely related concepts. Mercy according to the bible is the unmerited goodness, or love of God, to those who have forfeited it, and are by nature are under a sentence of condemnation, and the goodness or love of God shown to those who are misery or distress, irrespective of their deserts. In order words, God withholds the judgment and condemnation we actually deserve. Erickson expresses it in this way: "God deals with his people not on the basis of their merit or worthiness, what they deserve, but simply according to their needs. On the other hand, he deals with them on the basis of his goodness and generosity. God performs undeserved favors for his people. God's mercy is not a temporary or mood, but an attribute of God's being. God has always been gracious and merciful-as shown throughout the Old Testament {Luke 1:50}.

Grace on the other hand, involves God imputing merit "Where none previously existed and declares no doubt to be where one had been before . . . Grace is the good pleasure of God that inclines him to bestow benefits upon the undeserving. Indeed, grace is a gift from God {Eph. 2:8} which has been "lavished" upon us {Eph. 1:7-8}, and brings us salvation {Titus 2:11}.

GOD'S NAMES WHICH DEMONSTRATE HIS CHARACTER

The is what even some Christians, ask, are the names of the LORD GOD still effective, in order words, are they applicable in this dispensation?

They really forget that God never change. A friend of mine asked me one day, is not the book of Colossians 2:9 declares that "For in him dwells all the fullness of God? Then why do some Christians use other names of God in the process of prayer?

Hear me, beloved, the book of Malachi 3:6 portrays that God changes not, therefore what Jesus did not declare in the fulfillment of the Law is still applicable for the glory of God. All God's names are anointed and they are perfectly ever ready to accomplish all what they say they will do by faith. Apply the names in your prayer life and you will see the salvation of the Lord of host in your life.

1. JEHOVAH means:—The self existent One. In the book of Exodus, God made known his name to his servant Moses that he did not declare his name "JEHOVAH" to the Patriarchs but unto him, Moses. "And God spoke unto Moses, and said unto him, I am the Lord. And I appeared unto Abraham, unto Isaac, and unto Jacob, by the name of God Almighty, but by my name JEHOVAH was I not known to them" {Exodus 6:2-3}.

2. JEHOVAH-NISSI means:—The Lord of War. The Lord God declared himself as a God who shields his people in times of warfare against his enemies. God sworn to Moses that he would fight the enemies of his people from generation to generation. "And Moses built an altar, and called the name of it "JEHOVAH-NISSI: For he said, because the Lord has sworn that the Lord will have "war" with Amalek from generation to generation." {Exodus 17:15-16}.

3. JEHEVAH-RAPHA means the Lord who heals:—The Lord quenched the thirst of his people by healing bitter waters of Marah, in the wilderness of Shur, three days walk without water. The Lord proved them that "If you will diligently listen to the voice of the Lord your God, and will do that which is right in his sight, and will give ear to his commandments, and keep all his statues, I will put

none of these disease on you which I have brought on the Egyptians: for I am the Lord that heals you" {Exodus 15:22-26}

4. JEHOVAH—JIREH:—means the Lord will provide. He is the only "provision deity" which is able to provide more abundantly than ever on this planet. He makes a way where there is no way and hope, where there is no hope to his people who are obedient to him. He proved to Abraham that he is Lord of provision when he was to sacrifice son only son, Isaac unto him. "And Abraham lifted up his eyes, and looked and behold behind him a ram caught in a thicket . . . . And Abraham called the name of that place "Jehovah; as it is said to this day, in the mount of the Lord it shall be seen" {Genesis 22-13-14}

5. JEHOVAH SHALOM:—means the Lord of peace. Where there is tumor, catastrophic, and fearful, and war, it is only He can ensure peace in such situation. He declared to Gideon that he is the only Lord who can ensure peace in every situation life. "And the Lord said unto him Peace be unto you; fear not: you shall not die. Then Gideon built an altar there unto the Lord, and called it "JEHOVAH-SHALOM," unto this day it is yet in Ophrah of the Abiezrites.

6. JEHOVAH-SABAOTH:—means God Almighty who is a mighty military commander of host of angels who has dominion over all things. He vividly said to his people that he has the power to deal with his enemies. "Therefore, says the Lord, the Lord of Host, the Mighty one of Israel, Ah, I will ease me of mine adversaries, and avenge me of mine enemies." {Isaiah 1:24}.

7. JEHOVAH-TSIDKENU:—means Lord Our Righteousness. Righteousness is not achieved on the silver platter, or in order words, it is not what you think it righteous before your own eyes in godliness, but the Lord's. Outside the righteousness of the Lord of glory, every act of righteousness is not of God because He is our

righteousness. The Lord declared his name to Jeremiah the Prophet, "In his days Judah shall be saved, and Israel shall dwell safely; and this is his name whereby he shall be called "The Lord Our of Righteousness," {Jeremiah 23:6}.

8. JEHOVAH—SHAMMAH:—means the Lord is Present. Our abode is in the presence of the Lord whereby the righteousness shall give thanks to the Lord of glory, for his presence is our liberty. "It was round about eighteen thousand measures; and the name of the city from that day shall be, "The Lord is there".

9. JEHOVAH-M'KADDESH:—means the Lord Sanctifies. The cleansing of ourselves from all filthiness of the flesh and spirit, perfecting holiness in the fear of God is the Lord of Sanctification. "Speak thou also unto the children of Israel, saying, verily my Sabbaths ye shall keep; for it is a sign between me and you throughout your generations; that ye may know that I am the Lord that doth "sanctify" you. {Exodus 31:13}.

I hope this teaching will help you to understand the concept of God's nature. God is the same yesterday, today and forever more.

CHAPTER 9

DEITY OF JESUS CHRIST

INTRODUCTION

The doctrine about the deity of Christ Jesus has won much attention than any other topic in the history of mankind, scientific, academic and religious point of view. But I believe the Holy Spirit is going to help is with illumination to be able to come out with the true teachings by the end of the day to set the records straight for our utmost understanding of this unique concept. The following definitions are my summary of Bible teachings. I will not cite specific Scriptures at this point, but our study will show that these definitions fit Bible teachings.

"DEITY"—The essence or substance of God, The state or quality or condition of being God

"GODHEAD" is defined as the same as God.

"DIVINE" is the ability of possessing Deity; having qualities or characteristics possessed by God.

SCRIPTURAL PROOF THAT JESUS CHRIST IS GOD

As our society rapidly approaches the end-time events of the book of Revelation, Satan and his evil forces are doing everything within their power to deceive humanity and to condition men to worship an individual known as "the beast" or the "Antichrist" {Rev. 13:1-18}. Satan has always had a desire to be worshipped as God, {Isaiah 14:12; Luke 4:7}, and he will be worshipped as God in this coming Tribulation Period, {11 Thes. 2:3-4}. In order to bring this about, Satan realizes that he must first dethrone the true God in hearts and minds of people. That is, he must attack the Deity of Jesus Christ. This attack on the Lord Jesus Christ is being executed in many ways by many different groups, various cult groups, New Age groups, and even modern Bible translators have their own methods of robbing Jesus Christ of His Deity.

Many young men enter Bible colleges and seminars believing in the Deity of Christ, and then graduate four years later with less faith than when they were enrolled! What about you, friend? What do you believe about Jesus Christ? Can you support your beliefs with God's word? That is the real issue: what said the scripture? We challenge you to get your Bible {KJV} and check all the references that we are about to give. Note that the world is full of deception and don't ever allow yourself to be deceived by false teachers. Remember, Jesus is God Himself and not only the Son.

JESUS CHRIST IS GOD INCARNATE

Quoting from Isaiah 7:14, Matthew 1:23 says, "Behold, a virgin shall be with child, and shall bring forth a son, and they shall call his name Emmanuel, which is being interpreted as God with us." According to both of these verses, Jesus was "God with us" when He walked upon the earth. He was not merely "God's chosen one with us" or "God's Son with us." As 1 Tim. 3:16 states, "God was manifested in the flesh." John 1:14 tells us that, "the word was made flesh, and dwelt among us . . . ." In Zechariah 12:10, GOD said that HE {GOD} would be "pierced" by sinners, and Revelation 1:7 states that Jesus Christ Himself fulfilled this prophecy! Friend, the Bible presents Jesus Christ as much more than a prophet and teacher. God's word presents Jesus Christ as God incarnate.

DIVINE NAMES OF JESUS CHRIST

Check these references for yourself. In Matthew 22:42-45, Jesus claims to be the "Lord" of Psalm 110:1. He allows Thomas to address Him as "My Lord and my God" in John 20:28.

HE IS THE "EVERLASTING FATHER" AND "MIGHTY GOD" of Isaiah 9:6. According to his own words in John 10:11-14, he is the "Shepherd," of Psalm 23:1, Psalm 80:1, and Ezekiel 34:12.

GOD IS "SAVIOR" in Isaiah 43:3, 43:11, 45:15, 45:21, Hosea 13:4, Luke 1:47, and 1 Timothy 4:10, yet this title is given to Jesus Christ in Luke 2:11, Philippians 3:20, 11Timothy 1:10, and 11 Peter 2:20.

GOD IS "ROCK" of Deuteronomy 32:4, 32:15, 32:18, 32:30-31, 1Samuel 2:2, and Psalm 18:31, yet this title is given to the Lord Jesus Christ in 1 Corinthians 10:1-4, 1Peter 2:7-8, and Romans 9:33.

GOD IS "LIGHT" in Psalm 27:1 and Micah 7:8 and then Jesus is "light" in John 1:4:9 and in John 8:12.

In Isaiah 44:6, God says, ". . . . I am the first, and I am the last; and beside me there is no God." In Revelation1:17 Jesus Christ says, ". . . . Fear not; I am the first and the last." The scriptures are clear: Jesus Christ is the God of the Old Testament.

JESUS CLAIMED EQUALITY WITH GOD

Jesus say in Matthew 28:19, "Go ye therefore, and teach all nations, baptizing them in the name of the Father, and of the Son, and of the Holy Ghost." If Jesus Christ is not Deity, then why did He include Himself in the Holy Trinity?

Jesus says in John 14:9, ". . . he that has seen me has seen the Father; and how do you say then, show us the Father?" Is the Father someone other than Jesus Christ? No! Not according to Jesus Christ.

In John 10:30, Jesus says. "I and my Father are one." Is not that enough? Philippians 2:6 says that Jesus was in the "form of God", and that he thought it not robbery to be "equal with God"! The Jesus Christ of the New Testament claimed to be "one" with God and equal with God.

JESUS CHRIST IS OMNIPRESENT

Only God has the ability to be everywhere at once, yet Jesus claims this ability. In Matthew 18:20, he says, "For where two or three are gathered in my name, there I am their midst. How could this be possible if Jesus were not Deity? The same is true in Matthew 28:20 where Jesus says, . . . "lo I am with you always, even unto the end of the world. Amen." How could He be with each individual Christian always and be in heaven at the same time? He is God, for only God has such attributes.

JESUS IS OMNIPOTENT

That is, He is all powerful. He has all power. Revelation 19:6 states, ". . . the Lord God omnipotent reigns" then 1 Timothy 6:15 says that Jesus Himself is ". . . the blessed and only Potentate, then He must be the One of Revelation 19:6, God Almighty! Also see Colossians 2:26, and Matthew 28:18.

JESUS IS OMNISCIENT

To be omniscient, is to have all knowledge, unlike normal men. The Bible declares that Jesus was indeed omniscient. Jesus Christ had knowledge of specific details about His own death. In Matthew 16:21, Jesus said that He would go to Jerusalem, suffer many things at the hands of the scribes and the elders, be killed, and then be resurrected the third day. He repeat this prophesy in Matthew 29:19. Matthew 17:27 offers the account of Jesus knowing of a certain coin in a fish's mouth before the fish was caught!

He knew specific details about a woman's life whom He had never met {John 4:16-19}. He also had all knowledge about Nathaniel in John 1:47-49. Jesus Christ is Deity because He is omniscient.

JESUS HAS CREATIVE POWERS

John 1:1:-3 says, "In the beginning was the Word, and the Word was with God, and Word was God. The same was in the beginning with God. All things were made by him; and without him was not anything made that was made." The "Word" is the Lord Jesus Christ {John 1:14, 1John 1:1-3; 5:7}, and John 1:3 says, that all things were made by Him!

Colossians 1:16 says, ". . . by him were all things created . . ." Consider Hebrews 1:1-3, "God, who at the sundry times and in divers manners spoke in times past unto the fathers by the prophets, hath in these last days spoken to us by his Son, whom he hath appointed heir of all things, by whom also he made all worlds; who being the brightness of his glory, and the express image of his person, and upholding all things by the word of his power, when he had by himself purged our sins, sat down on the right hand of the Majesty on high." You see, by Jesus Christ, the worlds were made, and by Jesus Christ, all things are upheld. He has the power to create and sustain the universe.

JESUS CHRIST HAS THE POWER OVER THE ELEMENTS OF NATURE

In Matthew 14:25, Jesus literally walked upon the sea, and in Luke 8:24, he rebukes the wind and it obeys him. How could he perform such tasks if he were not God? It must be understood that Jesus did not pray for God to calm the sea; He calmed the sea Himself.

Because of his creative powers, all the elements submit to him, either in heaven, or on this earth, or under the earth. It was through him that all was created, {For by him were all things created, that are in heaven, that are that are in earth, visible and invisible, whether thee be thrones, or dominions, or principalities, or powers; all things were created by him, and for him," {Colossians 1:16}.

The reason behind is that, anyone who creates anything has the absolute power, or ability to manipulate it as he desires. So is Christ, the creator of the universe.

The question goes remains like this, so the body of Christ has the same ability to or power to control the elements in the universe? The answer is yes! How?

THE BODY OF CHRIST HAS POWER OVER THE ELEMENTS

Lets us recall what happened to the five kings of Amorites, the king of Jerusalem, the king of Jerusalem, the king of Hebron, the king of Jarmuth, the king of La' chish, and the king of Eglon, and all their hosts who gathered themselves before Gibeon and made war against it, {Joshua 10:5}. When the report was made known to Joshua he ascended from to fight on their behalf and Lord discomfited them before Israel and slew them with a great slaughter at Gibeon.

Gideon demonstrated the given power over the elements of the universe by commanding the moon and the sun to intervene in the battle against the enemy. God created everything before he created us according the book of Genesis chapter 1. The reason of us being the last creation is that we may come and have dominion and subdue over all things, {Genesis 1:28}, not only to take control over them, but also to enjoy them by using them to our needs.

With authority and power from the Lord of Host, Joshua, full of the Holy Ghost commanded the elements of Sun and moon to war against the enemy, and it was so. And Gideon said "in the sight of the Israel, Sun stand you still upon Gibeon; and you Moon, in the valley of Ajalon.

And the Sun stood still, and the moon stayed, until the people had avenged themselves upon their enemies" {Joshua 10:12b-13a}.

This authority has not been confined to a certain group of people but it is available us all. The only thing we need to do is to train our spiritual being to attain such power in the Lord. The body of have the same power in us to do exactly what Jesus did, like how he cursed the fig tree and it withered instantly, in the book of Mark 11:12-14.

In the Lord, we have every power and authority to take dominion over every element in the universe. Without him, we are incapable but take heart, he promised us that, "Verily, verily, I say unto you, He that believes on me, the works that I do shall he do also; and greater works than these shall he do; because I go to my Father," {John 14:12}. Beloved, stir up the gift within you, {2Timothy 1:6}, for you to reach that authoritative, and dominion, power apogee, given to us by the Lord.

THE BLOOD OF JESUS

SALVATION AND REDEMPTION

The phrase "blood of Christ" is used several times in the New Testament and is the expression of the sacrificial death and full atoning work of Jesus on our behalf. References to the Savior's blood include the reality that He literally bled on the cross, but more significantly, that He bled and died for sinners. The blood of Jesus Christ has the power to atone for an infinite number of sins committed by an infinite number of people throughout the ages, and all whose faith rests in that blood will be saved.

The reality of the blood of Christ as the means of atonement for sins has its origin in the Mosaic Law. Once a year, the priest was to make an offering of the blood of animals on the altar of the temple for the sins of the people. "In fact, the law requires that nearly everything be cleansed with blood, and without the shedding of blood there is no forgiveness" {Hebrew 9:22}. But this was a blood offering that was limited in its effectiveness that is why it had to be offered again and again. This was a foreshadowing of the "once for all" sacrifice which Jesus offered on the cross {Hebrews 7:27}. Once that sacrifice was made, there was no longer a need for blood of bulls and goats.

The blood of Christ is the basis of the New Covenant. On the night before he went to the cross, Jesus offered the cup of wine to his disciples and said, "This is the new covenant in my blood, Which is poured out for you"{Luke 22:20}. The pouring out of the wine in the cup symbolized the blood of Christ which would be poured out for all who would ever believe in him. When he shed his blood on the cross, he did away with the Old Covenant requirement for the continual sacrifice of animals. Their blood was not sufficient to cover the sins of the people, except on a temporary basis, because sin against a holy and infinite God requires a holy and infinite sacrifice. "But those sacrifice are an annual reminder of sins, because it is impossible for the blood of bulls and goats to take away sins" {Hebrew 10:3}. while the blood of bulls and goats were "reminder" of sin, "the precious blood of Christ, a lamb without blemish or defect" {1Peter 1:19} paid in full the debt of sin we owe to God, and we need to further sacrifice for sin. Jesus said, "It is "finished" as he was dying, and he meant just that-the entire work of redemption was completed forever, "having obtained eternal redemption" for us {Hebrew 9:12}.

THE IMPORTANCE OF THE BLOOD OF JESUS

Because of the blood of Christ shed on the cross we have

* Redemption
* Justification and the
* Forgiveness of sins and peace with God, which come when we turn from sin and place a faith in Jesus that will trust and obey

him. We contact Jesus' blood, in a spiritual way, when we repent and place a submissive faith in him. Jesus precious blood also:

* Cleanses our consciences so we may serve God,
* Makes us a holy,
* Purifies us from sin,
* Frees us from sin,
* Is what purchased us for God {if we are true Christians},
* Washes white our spiritual robes,
* And is the means of overcoming the devil along with the word of our testimony and not loving our lives so much as to shrink from death.

Clearly, the blood of Jesus Christ shed on the cross is necessary for one to have salvation. But that is not all. Scripture declares something else. In heaven, they sing to Jesus about his blood and what it has accomplished.

THE BLOOD AS A SPIRITUAL WEAPON

There have been many instances whereby the blood has delivered many children of God from the clutches of the enemy. The devil couldn't stand when the blood of Jesus was pronounced against him by the archangel Michael and his host of angels in heaven. The book of Revelation reveals that Satan was thrown out from heaven by the blood of the Lamb of God. "And they overcame him by the blood of the Lamb and by the word of their testimony; and they loved not their lives unto the death." {Revelation 12:11}.

"As for you also, because of the blood of your covenant, I will set your prisoners free from the waterless pit" {Zechariah 9:11}. Can you please understand exactly what the Lord is telling you? Then hear me, the Lord is saying that because you of the covenant of the blood which was shed for the redemption of the humanity, including you, he will look at the shedding of the blood to redeem you from every snares and shackles of the enemy in your life. The redemption purposes is done away only by the blood, therefore your freedom of life from the clutches of the enemy depends how apply the blood of the Lord in your life, not only your life but your family and your business.

What did the book of Ephesians say about our redemption purposes in our daily life. Watch this, when we sin, we become slaves of sin, "Know you not that to whom you yield yourselves servants to obey, his servants you are to whom you obey, whether of sin unto death, or of obedience unto righteousness? {Romans 6:16}. And "He that commit sin is of the devil" {1John 3:8}. And who causes sin which leads to death? If you do believe that it is the devil, then the Bible is telling you in the book of Ephesians that "In whom we have redemption through his blood" {Ephesians 1:7}.

Never feel reluctant in your daily life to apply the covenant blood which was shared for redeeming you from any prison in your life be the enemy of progress. It is will be a great testimony in your life if you begin to apply the blood. Your watch word is, "if you are willing and obedient, you will eat the good of the land, but if you resist and rebel, you will be devoured by the sword, for the mouth of the Lord has spoken" {Isaiah 1:19-20}.

A certain witch one time told me that a Christian who cannot be manipulated by the forces of darkness is the one who is blood washed and at the same time covered with the blood. I would like you to put this into practice when you usually have nightmares when asleep. You see, when asleep, it is automatically that the dark world would visit you to steal and to destroy you. Therefore, the only way to overcome them is to apply the blood over your spirit, because you are a spiritual being {Genesis 2:7}, body, and the soul. Whenever you are about to sleep apply the blood of the Lamb and you will see the salvation of the Lord in your night vision.

I have a great testimony which I would like to share with you. God demonstrated to me how powerful the blood of the Lamb of God destroys the works of the enemy. In my night vision, I saw a very short woman who walked towards me frightened. All of sudden, she went back and prepared for my destruction unknowingly. Without hesitation, she rushed towards me to attack me, and I heard a voice behind me saying "Plead the blood of the Lamb of God against her, and she will be destroyed." I obeyed the voice and applied the blood of Jesus, and the victory was my portion, finally.

Amazingly, I saw the whole body of the short lady divided into pieces on the floor, like a bomb was planted in her body for destruction. I finally knew that the blood of Jesus was a powerful weapon to annihilate the camp of the enemy as the book of Revelation 12:11 revealed to us.

Beloved, what I have seen and hear is what I declare to you. The blood of the Lamb of God is a spiritual weapon which every child of God should apply in their daily lives.

Really, the blood of Jesus Christ shed on the cross is necessary for one to have salvation of our sins and iniquities. It has a great impart against the forces of darkness, and to deliver us from the schemes and all the snares of the fowlers.

CHAPTER 10

THE MIGHTY HOLY SPIRIT

"Go therefore and make disciples of all nations, baptizing them in the name of the Father, and the Son and the Holy Spirit," {Matthew 28:19}. "The grace of our Lord Jesus Christ, the love of God, and the fellowship of the Holy Spirit, be with you all" {11 Cor. 13:14}. Although the verse gives us no information of 4th century Trinitarian doctrine of "three in one" etc, it most certainly proves the Holy Spirit is a weapon. To suggest we are to be baptized in the name of {or by the authority of} the Father, the Son and electricity, and assaults of our common sense. Three persons are clearly implied in this verse. With 11Cor 13:14, like Matthew 28:19, we have a three part combination verse that demands grace, love and fellowship be equally ascribed to three corresponding persons.

WHAT IS A PERSON

Definition of person: "One who had substance, completeness, self-existent, individuality and rationality.

Five tests to determine a person:
Substance: being existence reality
Completeness: that which is part does not satisfy the definition {an arm}
Self-existent: continued by one's self, not by another: robot
Individuality: not some universal existence
Rationality: excludes the nonintellectual rocks and plants
Is the Holy Spirit an "it" or a "H"? Jn 16:12-14

THE HOLY SPIRIT IS SIMPLY A PERSON

The Holy Spirit is outright said to have a mind which energy does not.

Romans 8:27 He has a mind. {The Father who searches the heart of man knows the mind of the Holy Spirit who intercedes}.

The Holy Spirit experiences emotions, slights and injuries which energy does not.
Mt 12:31 "blaspheme against the Holy Spirit? {blaspheme against energy?}
Hebrew 10:29 "and have insulted the Spirit" {insult energy?}
Acts 5:3 "you have lied to the Holy Spirit" {lie to energy}

The foregoing pinpoints that the Holy Spirit is not energy but a deity as God who can be fellowshipped, who has thoughts and can speak, who is our advocate and intercedes for us, who share the same qualities with the Father, the Son in power, and having the same divine in character in the Godhead.

Some Christians do have in mind that the Holy Spirit is just an active force which God the Father uses for his works. No! is the answer. He is God himself and He does what he will, {1Cor. 12:11}. He has all authority and power to execute what pleases him in his operations in the universe. He has the authority as the Father and the Son because they are all one in heaven, "For there are three that bear record in heaven, the Father, the Word which is the Son, and the Spirit," {1Jn. 5:7}.

The Holy Spirit has the same attributes like the Father, and the Son. He is Eternal, Omnipresent, Omniscient, and Omnipotent. And He is the Almighty Creator of all things as Job 33:4 declared, "The Spirit of God has made me, and the breath of the Almighty gives me life."

THE RULING LORD OF LAST DAYS

Jesus said, "It is expedient for you that I go away: for if I go not away, the Comforter will not come unto you; but if I depart, I will send him to you." {John 16:7}. He came to glorify the name of Jesus, for Jesus said, "He shall glorify me; for He shall receive of mine, and shall show it to you" {John 16:14}.

We are going to talk about the God who is ruling this dispensation called, the Holy Spirit. The personal pronouns are use for Him as the gospel of John declared, "And I will pray the Father and He shall give you another Comforter, that he may abide with you forever" {John 14:16}, and read this also, {John 14:26}; {John 16:7-8}. He is self-existent: He moves and operates by one's self, not command by any other Deity.

THE CREATIVITY OF THE SPIRIT

Nothing will be accomplished in the operation of God without the movement of the Holy Spirit. God will not do anything without the Holy Spirit since the creation of the universe.

Before the creation, it was He the mighty One who has been operating all the creations of the universe. The word of God could not accomplish anything in the beginning till the operation of the Holy Spirit was manifested which can be recalled from the book of Genesis. Nothing was made manifest till He moved. "And the earth was without form, and void; and darkness was upon the face of the deep, and the Spirit of God moved upon the face of the waters" {Genesis 1:2}.

With this regard, God creates or operates through the power of the Holy Spirit in all his works on earth.

THE WORD AND THE SPIRIT: in the 11 Corinthians 3:17, the word of God say, "Now the Lord is that Spirit." The word of God will not go forth from the Lord without the movement of the Holy

Spirit. The moment the word is sent forth, the Spirit is already there for operation to glorify the name of Jesus. The triune God works in harmony, in heaven, and in the operation of mankind, in the kingdom of God on earth.

THE FELLOWSHIP OF THE HOLY SPIRIT

The major factor of the Christians today, not receiving all the blessings which the Father God has bestowed in our lives before the foundation of this world is the lack of fellowship with the Mighty Holy Spirit in these last days. Bear in mind that it his time of ruling the universe as Jesus declared in John 16:7. Therefore to receive all what you desire in the kingdom of God, you need to have a serious fellowship with HIM.

In order to have fellowship with him, you need to be baptized in the Holy Spirit, in order words, need to overflow in the Spirit in the inner most being. In the last day of the feast, Jesus stood and cried and said, "He that believes on me, as the scripture has said, out of his belly shall flow rivers of living water" {John 7:38}.

THE WAYS GOD BAPTIZED HIS PEOPLE IN THE HOLY GHOST

There are four ways God usually baptize his children with the Holy Ghost:

a. Some receive their Holy Spirit after being baptized in the water, right away coming out of the water. It means that they receive their Holy Spirit baptism after the water baptism at the right time.

b. Through dreams, many receive their Holy Spirit baptism. Many gifts are usually given by God in the dreams.

c. Impartations are on the rise to infuse the power of God to the children of God. It is good to receive the Holy Spirit baptism through impartations but the question is, do you think all the men of God in these last days are of God? Many false prophets are out there with demonic powers operating with the word of God.

d. The last but not the least is what God helped me through to receive my Holy Ghost baptism. In the book of Luke 11:13, Jesus said, "If you then, being evil, know how to give good food to your children; how much more shall your heavenly Father give the Holy Spirit to them that ask him?" it is a matter of prayer. When you pray sincerely to God, he will just give it to you as he did to me.

THE SPEAKING IN TONGUES

The subject of speaking in tongues has been a general argument in the church today. Some Christians believe it is all over, and others also believe this is the dispensation of the Holy Ghost which every child of God should speak in the kingdom of God. The question is, do you side with all over, or it should be spoken?, as a child of God? We are going to see if it is expedient for every Christian to speak in tongues or not.

THE PROPHECY OF SPEAKING IN TONGUES

The prophet Isaiah prophesied that a time would come whereby the Lord of host would speak to his people with tongues, "With stammering lips and another tongue will he speak to this people" {Isaiah 28:11}, and it came to pass in the day of Pentecost when Jesus told his disciples to wait till the receive power from on high at upper room. Many ministers speak against it, but there is no wonder, God knew that his people who are weary who need rest and refresh themselves in him will not embrace it, "To whom he said, this is the rest which you cause the weary to rest; and this is the refreshing; yet they would not hear" {Isaiah 28:12}. Beloved, I have been there and I do believe from my spirit that it is the greatest every child of God should pray for.

It is the door to possess all the blessings and riches of the kingdom of God. You may be asking yourself, why am I saying this? Hear me, know once and for all that the spiritual world rules the physical, and when you fail or don't prosper in the spirit, automatically, you have already failed in life.

We are spiritual beings having a soul, and living in the body, therefore, we have to live as spiritual beings in this world, "for we wrestle not against flesh and blood, but against principalities, against powers, against the rulers of the darkness of this world, against spiritual wickedness in high places" {Ephesians 6:12}. It is not by your might, or your power that you can overcome these beings, but rather it takes maturity in the spirit to overcome them, for they are all spiritual beings.

IN OUR DISPENSATION

Apostle Paul made an emphasis in the book of Corinthians 14:5 that "I would that

you all speak with tongues," {1Corinthians 14:5}. Please, can I really ask you a question? Whom is the word of God narrating to? Is it only the church at Corinth, or every child of God? God is speaking to everyone who is born again in his kingdom of light. Do not be blinded of what you have heard, but rather, what the word of God is speaking to your spirit. I would like to counsel you to be the doer of the word but not hearers only deceiving yourselves, {James 1:22}.

People marveled when they see the gifts of God being operated in the midst of his people. This cannot be achieved without being baptized in the Holy Ghost. Speaking in the tongues is a sign of being baptized in the Holy Ghost, as the Spirit give you an utterance. "And they were all filled with the Holy Ghost, and began to speak with other tongues, as the Spirit gave them utterance" {Acts 2:4}.

Peter declared it vividly that the speaking of tongues and the gifts of Holy Ghost is not meant to end at the Pentecost day with the apostles as some claim it to be. Most Christians argue that the tongues were meant for the early Christians alone, which is not true according to the book of Acts chapter 2:38, "Then Peter said unto them, Repent, and be baptized every one of you in the name of Jesus Christ for the remission of sins, and you shall receive the gift of the Holy Ghost, for the promise is unto you, and to your children, and to all that are far off, even as many as the Lord our God shall call."

The promise was not given unto those over there only, but rather it was extended to "those who are far off, even unto anyone who will believe in the Lord till he comes back for his bride. It to anyone who will come to the kingdom of God, then why do some argue that the baptizing of the Holy Ghost which gives utterance to the speaking of tongues is no more accepted in this dispensation?

THE REASONS WHY THE SPEAKING OF TONGUE IS ATTACKED

1. The language of speaking in tongues is not giving by men but rather from the throne of God, therefore, it has supernatural enablement which the devil and his cohorts can never understand it. It confounds the enemy when it is spoken because it carries all the spiritual dynamics which only the Lord understands the mind of the Spirit, {Romans 8:27}.

2. It shatters the plans of the enemy hidden against our lives and brings them into light. The good news is, may be you may plan to pray about your marriage or any issue which want the good Lord to do for you. The moment you start praying in the Holy Ghost, the Spirit will immediately know whatever is hidden from you by

the enemy, and He the Spirit will rather pray through you whatever is hidden from you to the Father, and it will be done right away to shame the enemy. It can be your issue or any of your relative whom the Lord would like you to pray for to deliver, The Bible says, "We know not what we should pray as we ought; but the Spirit itself makes intercession for us with groaning which cannot be uttered" {Romans 8: 26}.

3. There is a great mystery when the people of God gather in the prayer meetings. The is issue is that in every meetings like that, the agents of the enemy also show up to disrupt what the people desires from God, and what the Lord also has for his people. What happens in the course of the prayer is that the moment, as the people of God pray, the demonic agents whom you see physically as brothers and sisters in the Lord will swallow all what you may pray to the Lord. You might be asking, in what way? The moment the people start to pray, these agents open their mouths spiritually to swallow whatever prayer they want to swallow. It depends whom the forces of darkness have targeted to deal with from the kingdom of darkness. But when you pray in the Holy Ghost, beloved, it mounts directly to the throne of God without any rebel holder against your prayer, and the Spirit will make intercession for you according to the will of God, {Romans 8:27}.

THE IMPORTANCE OF THE PRESCENCE OF THE HOLY GHOST IN OUR LIVES

If the children of God know the importance and benefits of the overflowing of the Spirit of God, they will not hesitate to seek for it. The following are the benefits of the baptism of the Spirit of God, which leads us to the presence of God overflowing in us.

1. OUR FELLOWSHIP IS GRANTED IN HEAVEN:—How can a natural minded have a sound communion with the God who is a Spirit? Spirit deals with the Spirit and natural to natural.

The book of John 4:24 declares that, "God is a Spirit; and they that worship him must worship him in spirit and in truth." The only accepted fellowship with the Father is to be in the spirit and not carnal, for "For to be carnally minded is death; but to be spiritually minded is life and peace, because the carnal mind is enmity against God; for it is not subject to the law of God, neither indeed can be. So then they that are in the flesh cannot please God." {Roman 8:6-8}.

2. THE CURSE OF THE LAW IS BROKEN:—it takes the Spirit to fulfill the keeping of the law, for when one is offended, the whole law is broken, {James 2:10}. The Lord therefore sent us the Spirit of truth, so that we can abide in his truth in "love" which sums up the whole commandments. When the love of God is perfected in us, the curse of the law is no more existence in our lives, and that the blessing of Abraham might come on the gentiles "us" through Jesus Christ; that we might receive the promise of the Spirit through faith." {Galatians 3:14}.

3. THE LIFE OF CHRIST IS MANIFESTED IN OUR BODY:—The book of Psalms 16:11 declares that "in his presence there is fullness of joy." The greatest part of experience in life is to possess the life of Christ manifested in your body, that is, the presence of God. When the presence is manifested in your body, no demon from the pit of hell can approach you for manipulations.

4. ALL THE PROMISES OF GOD BECOME YOURS:—When you are overflowing in the Holy Ghost, you became a heir to all the promises of God because you are no more a child or a servant, but rather a son who is the heir of the promises, Galatians 4:1-2}.

5. YOU WILL BECOME A PARTAKER OF A DIVINE NATURE:—When you are plunged in the divine nature, all

the blessings of God in Christ Jesus become your portion. We share equally with the Lord what ever the God the Father has bestowed on his dear Son, {Roman 8:17}. Every thing the Father has spoken concerning his dear Son you will become a co-heir to Christ and you will be a partaker of the divine nature.

6. THE THRONE OF THE DEVIL IS DESTROYED:—Prayer vanquished the schemes of the devil but the most vital tool which Satan cannot approach to manipulate the people of God is the presence of the Mighty Holy Spirit. When the presence of the Holy Spirit or the presence of Christ, show forth in one's body, the schemes of the devil are put into naught.

7. OUR PRAYERS ARE HEARD IN THE TRONE OF GOD:—Pray in the Spirit is essential in our lives, for God knows the mind of the Spirit {Roman 8:27}. Spirit to spirit and deep call to deep, which intercedes on our behalf of things we do not even know to pray about. The Spirit knows our immediate needs which are ignorant of, and therefore transfer all our secret needs to the mercy seat of God.

9. THE CALL OF GOD IS ESTABLISHED:—Many could not fulfill their calling from God because of the lack of the spiritual enablement. To pay the price has made many difficult to move in the Spirit. Without being full in the spirit you cannot do all what God calls you to do because the kingdom of God comes with power, {Mark:1}, but not with carnally attitudes of eating and drinking, "For the kingdom is not meat and drink; but righteousness, and peace, and joy in the Holy Ghost," {Romans 14:17}.

THE HOLY SPIRIT QUICKENS OUR DEAD BODIES

Sicknesses and diseases are not our portion as heavenly born sons and daughters of God. Sicknesses and diseases came about when men over rule the commandments of the Lord. The law was given to the people of God to enjoy the life which the Lord God has ordained for his people. The law which was life given, therefore became death when men sinned against the commandment of God, so death brought sicknesses and diseases into our bodies when men did not hearken to the commandments of God through sin, "But it shall come to pass, if you will not listen to the voice of the Lord your God, to observe to do all his commandments and his statutes which I command you this day; that all these curses shall come upon you, and overtake you" {Deuteronomy 28:15}.

It takes the Mighty Holy Spirit to deliver us from the law of sin and death through the redemptive purposes of the cross of Calvary. An apostle Paul declared that, "For the law of the Spirit of life in Christ Jesus has made me free from the law of sin and death, for what the law could not do, in that it was weak through the flesh, God sending his own Son in the likeness of sinful flesh, and for sin, condemned sin in the flesh" {Romans 8:2-3}.

THE DWELLING PLACE OF THE MIGHT ONE

Can the holy God reside with the infirmities? No! But we have allow it and have accepted is as normal in the kingdom of God, which is contrary to the message Jesus gave in the book of Luke, "He has sent me to heal the brokenhearted, to preach deliverance to the captives, and recovery of the sight to the blind, and to set at liberty them that are bruised, "{Luke 4:18}.

The curse of the law pronounced in Deuteronomy was broken when Jesus cried out, "It is finished." {John 19:30}. Is it only the wealthy blessings of Abraham which the bible says it should "come on the gentiles through Jesus Christ; that we might receive the promise of the Spirit through faith," {Galatians 3:14}. That is not! The prosperity of our health is the major factor which the Bible talks about, for it is written, "Beloved I wish above all things that you may prosper and be in good health, even as your soul prospers" {1Jn 1:2}. How can you be a wealthy child of God whereas you are suffering in your body?

The Lord has given us a key to overcome sicknesses and diseases in his word which we are going to share. If the people of God are to respond to what has been accomplished for them on the cross through the law of the Spirit of life in Christ Jesus, the children of God would be prospered and be in good health.

WE ARE THE HOUSE

"Know ye not that ye are the temple of God, and that the Spirit of God dwelleth in you" {1Corinthians 3:16}. As the house of the living God, our bodies are to enjoy the presence of the God every moment and at anytime, because the triune God abode in our bodies. Many Christians get sick, for the lack of the presence of the Holy Ghost in their bodies. Get this straight, before the presence is manifested in the body, there might be fire burning inside the inner most being, and where there is fire every unwanted materials are to burn up. The book of Romans made it vividly to us that, "But if the Spirit of him that raised up Jesus from the dead dwells in you, he that raised up Christ from dead shall also quicken your mortal bodies by his Spirit that dwell in you," {Romans 8:11}.

The Lord says, he will make alive any part of the body which is not functioning as it is suppose to be, and any infirmity cannot live in the body because of the presence of the power of the Holy Ghost being fully charged in the body.

Beloved, the only way to enjoy sickness free in your body is to seek for the presence of the Mighty Holy Spirit in your life, "For the kingdom of God is not meat and drink; but righteousness, and peace, and joy in the Holy Ghost." {Romans 14:17}.

DIVINE TITILES AND NAMES OF THE HOLYS SPIRIT

The Spirit of life, {Eze. 37:1-10: Jn 6:63}
The Spirit of the Lord Jehovah, {Isaiah 61:1-3}

The Spirit of Holiness, {Rom 1:4}

The Oil of Gladness {Heb 1:9}

The Holy Spirit of Promise {Eph 1:13}

The Spirit of Jesus Christ {Phil 1:19}

The Spirit {Jn 20:22}

The Spirit of the Living God {2Cor 3:6}

The Spirit of Burning {Fire}{Mat 3:11}

The Spirit of God {1Cor 3:16}

The Spirit of Burning {Isaiah 4:3-4}

The Spirit of Judgment {Isaiah 4:4}

The Spirit of His Son {Gal 4:6}

The Spirit of Glory {1Peter 4:14}

God {Acts 5:3-4}

The Spirit of Life {Romans 8:2}

The Spirit of God, and of Christ {1Cor 3:16, Rom 8:9}

The Eternal Spirit {Heb 9:14}

The Spirit of Grace {Heb 10:29}

The Spirit of Wisdom and Knowledge {Isa 11:2}

The Spirit of Jehovah {Isa 11:2}

The Holy Spirit {Lk 11:13}

The Spirit of Grace and Supplication {Zech 12:10}

The Comforter {Jn 14:26}

The Spirit of Truth {Jn 14:17, 15:26}

CHAPTER 11

THE CALL BY GOD

The call of God is divinely inspired, but not a man's philosophical ideologies which end up with confusion and chaos in the course of the ministration. You can't just wake up and say I am going to do the work of work without being called by God. We don't enter in the calling because we feel like doing something for God because it is very dangerous if not called by God. Before he would call you, know for sure that you were predestined before were brought to this world. "And those he predestined, he also called; those he called, he also justified; those he justified, he also glorified" {Romans 8:30}.

Before God calls you into a ministry, he will equip you with that ministerial gift "for the work of ministry, for building up the body of Christ" {Ephesians 4:12}. You cannot enter into the ministry because someone tells you that you can make it or your actions and your speech qualifies or suit you to do it, no! That is outside of God's plan of calling into the ministry. God "will not sustain you to the end" 1Cor 1:8 to the end of the ministry because he has not called you, but rather you called yourself.

Sometimes, some ministers make mistakes in the time of the ministry. They usually think that because the can train their wives to know the word of God, they push them as ministers of the gospel whereas they have {wives} have not been called by God to minister, and Satan enter therein to cause confusion in the ministry. Therefore, husbands, if you have been called by God, don't try to make a preacher out of your wives. And the same thing applies to the women who have been called by God to minister, don't make a preacher out of your husband.

The personal call to ministry can be confusing. There are no Damascus flashes, no handwriting on the wall, no angels appearing with cryptic messages. So what is it? What is God's call of individuals into ministry? How does it work and how can you know for sure? This bible study will address these questions. Bring your notes to school as we will discuss this topic together.

Is there a common calling for all believers? Yes! In the following verses, discover and write out how the passage reveals that all believers are called to . . .
Salvation,{Roman 8:30}
Sanctification, {2Timothy 1:9}
Service {2Corinthians 5:20}

WHAT IS A CALL FROM GOD

The definition we use is, "An identifiable spiritual purpose or objective for your life." if that is true, what critical question is answered for you by understanding God's calling on your life?

To what does God call people? How does God He call people? What means does He use? Look up the following verses and record the answers to each. For the second column, write "P" if God called that person to a specific place, "L" if to a life-long ministry, and/or "T" if to a specific task. The first one has been completed for you

Rather than a burning bush or a voice in the night, the "call" today may come like Nehemiah's, as a burdened heart, or like Paul's, or from God through the words of a believer or perhaps God has spoken to you through his word. Regardless of how he called you, he has planted a desire to use your God-given gifts and abilities to further his kingdom building here on earth. Seriously considering where he would have you serve is a response to the will of God.

YOUR PERSONAL CALL TO MINISTRY

How do you know God's calling on your life? Think through the following, look up the passage, and write your answers. Have I spent time in prayer over this? Prayer should govern all aspects of a believer's life, so it is not unrealistic to begin discerning God's will for service in prayer. Has God used any particular passage of scripture to call me to his service? Since God speaks to us today through his word, he may use a scripture passage that addresses the very area of ministry that he is calling you to.

HOW IMPORTANT DO I SENSE THIS MINISTRY

Study Philippians 3:14, and meditate on the meaning of "high calling." To sense your calling in this respect, the following must be put under consideration

Do I have the approval of my spiritual leaders?

Study Acts 13:1-3, consider the role of the spiritual leaders in the calling of Paul and Barnabas, and think about how this model can relate to you and give you direction.

Have I seen God use me in this?

Read John 15:16. This passage adds another perspective to knowing the calling of God in your life.

End this study with a personal statement that indicates what you believe God is calling you to, and why you believe that, based upon what you have learned. Don't forced yourself into ministry and allow God to call you at his own appointed time.

HOW TO DETERMINE THE CALL
OF GOD UPON YOUR LIFE

God's calling to ministry is not authoritative the way the scriptures are. Your calling is never beyond question. You cannot claim it to others the way you quote scriptures to them. Nevertheless, our calling can be profoundly and durably sure in our own hearts. It is the work of God to bring our hearts to a point of conviction that, all things considered including scripture, this path is the path of obedience. The conviction is not infallible. But when it is of God, it brings peace.

To determine a divine calling in your life, know with certainty that God deals with our spirits as we are spiritual beings having souls and living in bodies. And the Holy Spirit lives inside our spirits so God works through us, in our spiritual beings. Therefore, we can hear from God inside us when he quickens our spirit and reveals to us his plans concerning our calling. If you are not convicted that you have been called by God to the ministry and you want the Lord to tell you, here is your solution.

Worship the Lord, and pray earnestly, and listen to your inner intuition, then you will hear the still small voice inside of you, telling you what to do, "And your ears shall a word a word behind, saying, this is the way, walk in it, when you turn to the right hand, and when you turn to the left" {Isaiah 30:21}. You will then feel a divine compulsion inside of you only if have made decision to be fully and consecrated to God to do anything he wants you to do for his glory.

The question remains that, how does God waken such a calling? I will suggest ten means that he uses. Only one of these is infallible, the Bible. All others are relative. They are not absolutely decisive in your leading. They are important. But any of them can be overridden by the others. Various combinations of these are the fuel God uses to drive the engine of his calling in your life.

1. Above all, know your Bible and saturate your mind with it

The Bible shapes our minds, for mission durability {Psalm 1:1-3}, and makes us burn for Christ {Luke 24:32}}.

2. Know your gifts and know yourself

Every Christian has a gifts {1Peter 4:10-11}. Knowing them shapes your convictions about your calling. And knowing yourself {as Paul exemplifies in Romans 7:15-24} deepens your sense of fitness for various ministries. {keep in mind that this can be overridden by other facts!}.

3. Ponder the need of the world

The Christian heart of love is drawn by perceived needs, whether near or far. Therefore, God uses what we know to awaken the measure of our desire that pushes us over the edge of commitment, {Matthew 9:36-38}.

4. Read missionary biography and missionary frontline stories

Clearly, Bible treats heroes of the faith as divinely appointed inspirations for the awakening of vision and ministry, {Hebrews 13:7}. "Therefore, since we are surrounded by so great a cloud of witnesses, let us also lay aside every weight, and sin which do so easily beset us, and let us run with patience the race that is set before us, {Hebrew 12:1}.

5. Inquire of your soul, "Where are you burdened for others"

God sends and seeks the burden for lost souls, Jesus carried such a burden; "O Jerusalem, Jerusalem! . . . . How then would I have gathered your children together as a hen gathers her brood under her wings" {Luke 13:33-34}. This burden was essential to his calling. What is your burden?

6. Know your circumstances

To become a minister of God, you must vividly understand the circumstances surrounding your call. "Truly, I say to you, there is no one who has left house or brothers or sisters or mother or wives or father or children or lands, for my sake and for the gospel, who will not receive a hundredfold now in this time, houses, and brothers, and sisters, and mothers, and children, and lands, with persecutions and in the world to come eternal life" {Mark 10:29-30}.

7. Pray the Lord to throw you where you can be best used for his glory

I say "throw" because in Matthew 9:38 that is the literal meaning; "Pray earnestly to the Lord of the harvest to throw out laborers into the harvest." The point is pray! Ask God to use you to the fullest of his glory, "If anyone lacks wisdom, let him ask God, who gives generously to all without reproach, and it will be given him" {James 1:5}.

8. Do not neglect passionate, Christ exalting, corporate worship

The most important missionary calling that ever happened took place in corporate worship; "while they were worshiping the Lord and fasting, the Holy Spirit said, set apart for me Barnabas and Saul for the work to which I have called them" {Acts 13:2}.

9. Listen humbly to the spiritual people in your life

Do not only confirm your gifts. They are the instruments of God to awaken in you possibilities and joys of missionary service that you never dreamed {2 Timothy 1:5-7}.

10. Cultivate absolute surrender of all you are and have to Christ

This is the person that God leads to the greatest fruitfulness of life. Woe to the person who tries to be a half-Christian and never says from the heart; "I renounce everything for you, Lord Jesus. I am willing to go anywhere and do anything at any cost, if you will, go with me and be my everlasting joy"

This is why Jesus said, "If anyone comes to me and does not hate his own father and mother and wife and children and brothers and sisters, yes, and even his own life, he cannot be my disciple. Whoever does not bear his own cross and come after me cannot be my disciple . . . Therefore, anyone of you who does not renounce all that he has cannot be my disciple" {Luke 14:26-27,33}.

WHY DOES GOD CALL US

I believe you understand with me that God does not call us for calling sake, but for a special purpose. The following are some of the reasons upon which God calls His people for service.

a. Salvation

Consider Matthew 9:12-13 "They that are whole need not a physician, but they that are sick. But you go and learn what that mean, I will have mercy, and not sacrifice; for I am not come to call the righteous, but sinners to repentance".

So God calls men and women, boys and girls every day for his divine enterprise. Therefore I believe God is knocking at the door of some one hearts. He is calling all those who are dying and on their way to hell. God is speaking to you right now so why don't you pay heed to His voice? God is calling you to the pool of His salvation. Jesus said no man cometh to the Father but by me. Come to Jesus for He is ready to save you.

b. He calls us to be saints

1Corinthians 1:2 "unto the church of God which is at Corinth, to them that are sanctified in Christ Jesus, called to be saints, with all that in every place call upon the name of Jesus Christ our Lord, both theirs and ours."

In order words, He doesn't call you to salvation just to fold your arms doing nothing. When you saved by the grace of God, you become a new creature. Old things have passed away and all things have become new.

He wants us to know who are as God's people and He has called us into the family of His saints. The Bible makes it emphatically clear that we are a peculiar people and a holy nation through the atonement of Jesus Christ on the cross. We are saved and our names are written in the book of life which is sealed by the power of the Holy Spirit. You are in the family of God's saints. Therefore, He wants you to bring others to come and part of this great family through the gospel of Christ.

c. To be separated unto Him

The bible teaches us that we are a chosen people, a royal priesthood, a holy nation, a people belonging to God that you may declare the praises of Him who called you out of darkness into the wonderful light. 1Peter 2:9. This divine of God has made us to move from the camp of slavery to son ship. You are indeed a special person in the Lord; therefore, you should be an example to others by being a person without blemish in order to have a perfect ministry for the accomplishment of His divine purpose upon you in His kingdom.

d. To fulfill His Purpose

The primary purpose of God for calling us a Christian is to fulfill His purpose of preaching the gospel of Christ to mankind and to cater for

His flock. Therefore, we will have a case to answer if we fail to do so. Accepting His invitation to become His son as an approved servant of God who is willing to do His will, you are obliged to evangelize to the world. We are saved and washed clean by the precious blood of His beloved Son to become the preachers of His gospel. The writer of the book of Hebrews says;

"Therefore do not be ashamed of the testimony of our Lord, nor of me His prisoner, but share with me in the sufferings, for the gospel according to the power of God, who has saved us and called with a holy calling, not according to our works, but according to His own purpose and grace which was given to us in Christ Jesus before time began" {11 Timothy 1:8-9}.

It pays to do the work of God because I don't know where I would have being without working for Him as His humble servant.

e. To Become Servants Of Christ

This is one of the teachings many ministers of God today don't want to hear, because they prefer the word "boss" to a mere servant. But we should not forget that our Lord Jesus Christ paid a high price on us with His own blood to redeem us from the slave market of sin to be acceptable in the kingdom of God. Therefore, we are free men in the world but slaves in his business of the gospel;

"For he who is called in the Lord while is the Lord's freeman, likewise he who is called while free is Christ slave . . ."{1Corinthians 7:22-23} {1Corinthians 6:19-20}.

As Paul in this regard calling himself a slave of Jesus at this point has a lot to do with the common custom of the Jews in the Old Testament era. By if a slave finished his serving time under his master, he was set free and allowed to move on with his life but for the love for his master he can decide to serve him for the rest of his life. This means that he had he had chosen not to accept his freedom and when this happened, he received a mark pierce on his ear. And when this sign was given, he is identified as a "love slave" for his master for life. Exodus 21:5-6, Deuteronomy 15:16-17}. Here, Apostle Paul by choice made himself a love slave for Our Lord Jesus for life.

Accepting this divine calling of God has automatically made you a slave {servant} under His authority to serve His flock and not to be served by the flock. My word of advice to all ministers of God is that they are called to be servants by mending His flock and not to be seen by the congregation as super humans.

f. To Do His Will

This is yet another area many church leaders get confused with. They easily adore and cherish the various offices and gifts under the five-fold ministry and the spiritual gifts than the responsibilities they come with. I don't this should be a problem at all. The fact is that just as Apostle Paul had a special calling upon himself, so do you and I. it is sparkling clear that Paul was called to be an apostle, but there were many people with different offices and gifts who also carried on with their callings and various offices for the building of the early churches, Romans 12:3-8, Ephesians 4:7-16.

We should get it straight that the various calling upon us are offices with responsibilities but not titles as many people presume. All we need is just honesty and patience, for the special part that God wants us to play in the building of His kingdom and I believe it will be reveal to us if only we still listen to His voice.

BE SERIOUS TO THE MINISTRY

It is evident that you have been called, but ask yourself, am I ready for the Lord to us me,? "Do not be deceived; God cannot be mocked, a man reaps what he sows" {Galatians 6:7}. God knows you more than you do, so you need to set your self aside and say no to all the unworthy lives which is natural.

PERIOD OF PREPARATION

If really want the Lord to use you, there is a need to prepare your self both physically and spiritually. God will not just allow you to be in the field without being a man of the word of God. You have to study the word of God so that the will consume you and you also consume the word, "Study to show your self approved to God, a workman that needs not to be ashamed, rightly dividing the word of truth" {2Timothy 2:15}.

We are going to look at some of the things we should know and be vigilant about which will allow the Lord to use us for his purpose in our lives.

a. THE BAPTISM OF THE HOLY GHOST

Let me share this to you. There have been many ministers in the ministry who are doing the work of God naturally. What do I mean naturally? They are born again having the Holy Ghost in them but not overflowing with the Spirit of God, {the baptism of the Holy Ghost}. Without it, you will work outside of the plan of God.

b. DEDICATION

You have to make up your mind that you are totally committed to the work of God and nothing else. All your time must be given to the ministry only when you want the Lord to use you mightily for his glory. Say no to anything which can hinder you from giving all your time to the Lord.

c. DIE TO SELF

What do I mean die to oneself,? To die to oneself is totally deny yourself in anything of the world that gives you pleasure in life. I mean anything which the world offers you, to make you happy in life. Jesus made and emphasis about who can stand and be a good steward in his ministry given to us, "Then Jesus said to his disciples, whoever wants to be my disciple must deny themselves and take up their cross and follow me" {Matthew 16:24}.

e. CONSECRATION

God doesn't use any defile people who are not worthy before him. He is a holy God who does not look at sin. Why do you think Jesus cried on the cross "My God, my God why have you forsaken me" {Mat 27:46}. The reason is, he took the sin of all the humanity upon himself and became a sinner. God is expecting each one of us to live totally holy life before we can be a vessel to be used, because without holiness, no one can see God, {Heb 12:14}.

f. BE FERVENT IN PRAYER IN THE SPIRIT

Prayer is the key to every door in the kingdom of God. To aglow in the Spirit, God has given us direct way to communicate with him in the book of Ephesians 6:18, {Praying always with all prayer and supplication in the Spirit}. You might ask why in the Spirit? The reason is that when we pray in the Spirit, we grow more and more in the spirit, "He that speaks in an unknown tongue edifies himself" {1Cor 14:4}.

Beloved, the bible says "if you are willing and obedient, you will eat the good of the land, but if you resist and rebel, you will be devoured by the sword, for the mouth of the Lord has spoken" {Isaiah 1:19-20}.

CHAPTER 12

THE REVELATION OF THE MINISTERIAL GIFTS IN THE DREAM

INTRODUCTION

This area of the book is very important to every Christian, especially church leaders because it clearly reminds us of great commission given to the church. The term five fold ministry comes from Ephesians 4:11-12 "And he himself gave some to be apostles, some prophets, some evangelists, some pastors, some teachers, for the equipping of the saints for the work of ministry, for the edifying of the body of Christ,"

Jesus has given various ministry gifts to the church apostles, prophets, evangelists, pastors, and teachers. If the church is to be healthy it needs the influence of all these five fold ministerial gifts. Unfortunately, it is very rare to see this happening today. We need a resurrection of team ministry and a healthy balance of ministry gifts. And don't forget that these gifts were given to the church by Christ Jesus Himself according to the scripture.

I would like to talk a little about those whom God delights to be used as a vessel for his honor in this ministration of the five fold ministry and the gifts ordained in them. More of often, we would like the Lord speak loudly in our ears before we may believe that we have been given this gift or this ministry. Situations and conditions surrounding us sometimes deter us from the voice of the Lord so he reveals himself in the dreams, "For God speaks once, yes twice, yet man perceive it not" {Job 33:14}. When the stern warning or the message from the Lord is not perceived by his people, either he will channel it through his minister or in the dream.

Every given gift or ministry given to the body of Christ is usually revealed to us in the dream, which I am going to share with you.

WHAT IS A DREAM?

Dream is a series of thoughts, images, impressions or sensations revealed to man in the course of sleep. Dream is a channel through which God speaks to his children whiles we are asleep. When he visits us in the dream, he reveals to us the secret things which have been ordained in our lives and what the evil one has purposed in our lives.

HOW TO DIFFERENTIATE THE GODLY AND EVIL DREAM IN THE MINISTTRY

To begin with, our heavenly Father is a good God whose mercy towards endure forever, "For the Lord is good and his love endures forever, his faithfulness continues through all generations" {100:5}, and "No good thing will he withhold from them that walk uprightly" {Psalm 84:11}. And the book of Jeremiah 29:11, tells us that God has good plans towards our lives, plans to prosper and not to do us harm but to give us hope and a good future.

To know the ministerial dream descending from the throne of God, it has to align with the word of God, because God does not do anything apart from his word. The reason is that he created everything through his word, "All things were made by him, and without him was not anything made that was made" {John 1:3}. When you wake up from your dream, check and compare it to the word of God, if it goes in hand with the word of God, then it is godly. The reason I am saying this is that enemy sometimes comes like the angel of light to deceive us from the ministry which you have been called to do for the glory of God, therefore be vigilant in the voices you may hear and the dreams you may see in the dream.

MINISTRIAL GIFTS IN THE DREAM

I am going to share with you how God begun blessing me with any spiritual gift being manifested in my life. As I said earlier, the beginning of any ministry begin with the baptizing with the Holy Ghost. When you are full of the Spirit, the Holy Spirit always deals and reveals himself in the dreams concerning the ministry has born in your life. All the ministerial gifts the Lord has given me were revealed in the dreams.

Lot of things escape the people of God, just because we don't value our night visions which the Lord reveals to us concerning our life potentials. When I received the Lord in Israel, the Lord allowed me to see a lot of things in the dreams about who he is, how powerful it works against forces of darkness.

EVANGELISM

In two weeks of my regeneration into heavenly kingdom, I saw in a dream an old man with white long garment having a long staff. He called me and handled to me a bow with seeds in it. He therefore told me to go and sow them. When I wake up, the Holy Spirit ministered to me that I am called to evangelize the word of God, and I was not disobedient to that calling, {Acts 26:19}. The zeal of evangelism started burning in my heart like fire, and started to evangelize to the Jewish communities in Israel.

GIFT OF HEALINGS

In my dream, there appeared to me two ladies sitting in front of me talking unusual about someone else. And there appeared behind them that particular person. This scene suddenly disappeared and there came a certain man totally blind. I shook his shoulders and told him to stand beside me for a while. Another man also came after the blind man whose whole neck was covered with leprosy. Without delay, two ladies appeared on the scene praying fervently for the leper. I saw my self in front of the man and shouted "receive your healing in Jesus name", surprisingly, he shouted, "I am healed". Can you imagine what happen to me in that particular moment? All my fingers started burning when I woke up from my sleep till now. That was the gift of healings. Whomever I lay my hands, the fire of God will flow from me to the sick, and be healed.

It is not only healings, but also miracles have been wrought through me hands ever since. All these were revealed to me in the dreams. If only you will be attentive and check your dreams, then you will know that God has something for you in your daily dreams.

PROPHECY

The lord revealed to me in the dream to prophesy to a certain lady in the dream. in the course of the dream, I could not articulate the words but rather stammering, to the person throughout the whole prophesy. I therefore, woke up from the sleep. The Lord took me again to a certain man to prophesy. At this time, I made it correctly and it was marvelous to the glory of God. What can I say about this? It means that the Lord has given that gift for the benefit of the body of Christ.

There are a lot of things I can witness and talk about what the Lord has revealed to me in the dreams. But to let you know that there are good things in the dreams which the Lord reveals to his people who are called by his name

MINISTRIES REVEALED IN SYMBOLS

We are now going to study other dimensions which God reveals to us the ministries. He at times reveals to us in symbols. A lot of symbols have been revealed to me which I am going to share with you. In the dream I was going with Pastor Asia on a journey abroad, we later end up in the airport.

Without elaborating them all, I would like to single them out as follows:

a. Airport:—We go to air port to board a flight to abroad. So what can we align this to? This is the out going work of God called "missionary work".

b. Air plain:—Air plain goes from one place to another, either in the nation or outside the nation which implies evangelism.

c. Powerful engine:—Empowerment ministry of the Holy Ghost.

d. Hand holding a staff or a rod:—it is the office of a prophet.

e. Writing board:—office of teaching

f. Bus: Pastoral with a mega church

ABOUT THE AUTHOR

Rev. Alfred Johnson Mensah is indubitably one of the seasoned men of God of our time; who has touched millions of souls with his Pentecostal charisma and dynamisms through his teachings and writing since 1992 when he lost the world and the world also lost him.

Alfred who believed in the power of Satan by consulting several powerful fetish and occult fraternities for power came face to face with the dynamic power of Jesus Christ in Jerusalem-Israel when he traveled there for greener pastures in 1992. He finally accepted Christ Jesus as his Lord and personal Savior and was baptized in the red sea. The dramatic conversion of Rev. Alfred has made him one of the greatest healing and deliverance ministers of our time.

He is one of the men of God who preach the gospel of God with authority and he battles with Satan boot for boot through the power of the Holy Spirit upon him. Alfred has associate in theology from the bible church of Christ Institute in the Bronx New York. He is the founder and overseer of "Touch of Heaven Ministries" where God uses him to touch millions of souls with his Pentecostal charisma and dynamism with gospel of Christ. He is a healing and deliverance minister, and saints of God around the world speak highly of him and his ministry. The wonderful impartation of the Holy Ghost is emphasized in all his services and many miracles occur through his hands. The gifts of the Holy Ghost with demonstrations of power are manifested in his meetings as the Spirit of the Most-High God leads and empower him. He is indeed God appointed minister for this generation.

Currently, Rev. Alfred resides in the Bronx, New York with his family. Make a date with Jesus through this man and you will definitely make a date with your destiny.

BIOGRAPHY

This book and links listed are generally recognized as having perspective which merit the reader's consideration and are listed with the intention of providing a broad base of study.

A.W Tozer, the knowledge of the Holy {Carle, UK: OM Publishing, 1987}

I Berkhof, Systematic Theology {Edinburg: Banner of Truth, 1958}66

M. J. Erickson, Christian Theology, 2nd edition {Grand Rapids, Michigan: Baker, 1998}

H. C. Thiessen, Lectures in systematic theology {Grand Rapids, Michigan: 1979}

Lucifer: Father of Cain {LuLu.com. 2011}

Derek Price: Lucifer: Exposed {Whitaker House, 2006}

www. Sunrisedetox.com

www. Soberforever. Net

www. Christianity. About.com

www. Christianity. About.com

www. Godandscience.org/doctrine/who_is_satan.html

Write your notes

Write your notes

ARISE AND SHINE

Becoming God's Shining Star When the People Need the Light Most

The New Dawn Has Come
Shining Over Your Failure
The Light Doesn't Compromise with Sin
The Enemy of God's Shining Light
Prayer and Fasting
Understanding Church Leadership
The Light Brings Goals
The Nature of God
The Deity of Jesus Christ
The Deity of The Holy Ghost
The Call of God

"Arise and shine, for thy light has come, and the glory of the Lord is risen upon thee"

{Isaiah 61:1-2}

Through his own testimony and experience as a man delivered from the power of darkness, Rev. Alfred Johnson Mensah will bring you closer to God by showing you how many lives have been forever transformed through his ministry by the power of the Holy Spirit. Get in touch with this power healing and deliverance minister and have a date with destiny. Detailed information about him and his ministry is available in the last four pages of the book.